Robert Payne

Gershwin

Robert Payne

Gershwin

Illustrated

Brick Tower Press
Habent Sua Fata Libelli

Brick Tower Press
1230 Park Avenue
New York, New York 10128
Tel: 212-427-7139
bricktower@aol.com • www.BrickTowerPress.com

All rights reserved under the International and Pan-American Copyright Conventions.
Printed in the United States by J. T. Colby & Company, Inc., New York.
No part of this publication may be reproduced, stored in a retrieval system, or transmitted in any form or by any means, electronic, or otherwise, without the prior written permission of the copyright holder.
The Brick Tower Press colophon is a registered trademark of
J. T. Colby & Company, Inc.

Library of Congress Cataloging-in-Publication Data
Payne, Robert
Gershwin
Includes biographical references, index, and photos.
ISBN 978-1-883283-93-3

1. Payne, Robert— 2. Biography—George Gershwin 3. Performing Arts 4. Composers 5. Robert Payne Library, Volume 4.

Copyright © 1960 by Robert Payne

First Trade Paper Printing, April 2013
Gershwin

SABINA
With Love

Contents

		page
1	East Side, West Side	13
2	The Young Gershwin	18
3	Tin Pan Alley	28
4	Rhapsody in Blue	40
5	Portrait of a Composer on a High Trapeze	56
6	An American in Paris	72
7	The Wasted Years	82
8	Porgy and Bess	93
9	Death and Resurrection	107
	Select Bibliography	117
	Select Discography	119
	Index	123

Illustrations

		facing page
1	George Gershwin	32
2	Gershwin at the piano surrounded by theatrical celebrities: Jack Donohue, Marilyn Miller, George Gershwin, Sigmund Romberg and Florenz Ziegfeld	33
3	Scene from the Warner Brothers' film *Rhapsody in Blue*	33
4	George Gershwin standing by Walter Damrosch at the piano	48
5	Gershwin's self-caricature in the possession of Jules Glaenzer	48
6	George Gershwin at Los Angeles, 1937	49
7	*Porgy and Bess* at the Alvin Theatre, New York, October 1935	96
8	Todd Duncan, Anne Brown and John W. Bubbles in *Porgy and Bess*, 1935	97
9	George Gershwin in the middle 'thirties	97
10	Fred Astaire, George Gershwin and Ira Gershwin rehearse *Shall We Dance*, July 1937	112
11	Self-portrait	113

ACKNOWLEDGEMENTS

The above illustrations are copyright by the following: Francy and Company Limited (No. 1); Culver Pictures Incorporated (2, 4, 6, 7, 8 and 10); United Artists Associated Incorporated (3); Jules Glaenzer (5); the Associated Press Limited (9); and the Bettmann Archive (11).

Acknowledgements

THIS IS NOT so much an attempt to write a brief life of Gershwin as an account of the growth of a musician's mind. I have sought for the seeds of his actions and his music, hoping to discover what was important and true, and to uncover his motives, his feelings and origins. I have presented him as a tragic figure, because the stereotype of the "happy success story" seemed to me untenable and unworthy of him.

I knew him only through his music, and so it was necessary to interview those who still remembered him vividly. I am deeply grateful for the help I have received from Henry Cowell, Isamu Noguchi, Carl Van Vechten, Jules Glaenzer, Irving Caesar, John Farrar, Vinton Freedley, Patric Farrell, Kay Swift, Edgar Varèse, Robert Downing and Sholom Secunda, who introduced me gently to the Jewish theatre. I owe a special debt to Vernon Duke, who talked at length about Gershwin and permitted me to reproduce his account of Gershwin's death from his book, *Passport to Paris*, and to Dorothy Heyward, who gave me more of her time than I deserved and filled the air with her honeyed wisdom.

I

East Side, West Side

IN THE 1880s the Jews of New York were a race apart. They had their own way of life, their own food, their own shops and theatres. Most of them were Russian and Polish refugees from the pogroms which followed the assassination of Czar Alexander II. A peasant had killed the Czar, but the Jews were made to suffer; and as the pogroms grew worse, and the violence of the Procurator of the Holy Synod, who was the real ruler of Russia, increased, more and more Jews made their way to America. The Procurator had announced his programme—a third of the Jews must emigrate, a third must be baptized, and a third must be starved.

So they came in their hundreds of thousands to America, making their way in the holds of the immigrant ships, knowing very little English, terrified as all refugees are terrified by the prospects in store for them. Their roots were in the vast plains of Poland and the huddled ghettos of Russia; their memories were of the knout, the Cossacks, the stern "May laws" which flung them out of the homeland where they had lived for centuries. Rootless, they began to put down new roots in New York and in the towns on the eastern seaboard. They brought with them their own immemorial customs: a grave and sonorous ritual which penetrated their daily life. Without their Jewish heritage they could hardly have survived.

The lives of the Jewish immigrants in New York were filled with contradictions. While their Jewishness held them together, there were vast forces tending to split them apart; and while America was the land of opportunity, there were few opportunities open to the first generation of immigrants. These small traders and artisans and intellectuals seemed to have no place in the puritan traditions of America. They did not belong to the world of Horatio Alger. For the most part they were a humble people groping for a small place in the sun, only too conscious of the walls of hostility and indifference which surrounded them. To survive, they worked long hours in sweat-shops, lived in tenements and obeyed their Tammany bosses. "We are slaves," they told each other, "but our children will be doctors, lawyers, professors."

An authentic heroism buoyed up the spirits of the first generation of Jews to flee the pogroms. They saw little hope for themselves, but lived for the sake of their children, and they derived comfort from the richly embroidered ritual which they celebrated in the synagogues and in their homes. There were rituals for birth, for circumcision, for the first haircutting, for *bar mitzvah*, for marriage and for death, so that all the intimate details of family life acquired meaning and sanctity. On Friday evening the streets grew dark and there was always a hush of expectation, for after Friday came the Sabbath, "the bride," the day when all household duties, all work, all travel and traffic with money ceased. "The bride" was quietness, and the foretaste of heaven. There followed the long Saturday twilights when the delicatessen stores reopened, and life, which had been held in suspension, began again. Each week had its rituals, and the year was a long ritual interspersed with great festivals. Near Christmas there was the Festival of Lights, but the greatest moment of all was the one which introduced the Day of Atonement, the moment when the *Kol Nidre* was sung. On that tragic day the Jews abased themselves utterly before their God, finding peace and communion with their fellows in an act of total surrender.

But the synagogue was not the centre of Jewish life. The centre of life was the kitchen, which was far more than a place for cooking meals. The kitchen was where the family came together, where the mother presided in full matriarchal authority, and where the children were given their first instructions in the religious life. It was the place of the fading daguerrotypes on the walls, where bearded ancestors in skull cap and frock coat glared down on the huddled activities below. It was the place of the sewing machine, of the little trays of scissors and thread, of the porcelain jars filled with cookies and the bureau drawers full of long-forgotten passports and documents bearing the double-headed eagle of the czars. The kitchen was a garden enclosed, far from the garment factories and the rattling trolley cars, and here there was no necessity to speak the language of the *goyim*, that strange harsh tongue which was so difficult for the early immigrants to pronounce. Here life revolved around the mother, as the earth revolves around the sun.

Today it is difficult to visualize the warmth and vigour of those days, the seething crowds in the streets, the tramping of the dray horses on the cobblestones, the garish gaslight, the blare of the factory whistles, the ever-present smell of damp, the sawdust on the floors. There were whole streets which looked as though they had been transplanted bodily from Vitebsk or Lvov. Men dressed in long kaftans and broad-brimmed black hats, and many wore their hair in ringlets which dangled over their cheeks. The women, too, wore the costumes they had worn in Russia and Poland, and very few dared to wear the crinolines which were fashionable among the *goyim*. In those tenements tuberculosis was rampant, and in too many eyes there was the quick eagerness, the brightness, the leaping flame which comes from disease.

It was the time before people were driven silly by mass entertainments. There was no television, no phonograph, no radio. There might be a piano in the living-room, but there was entertainment enough in the family. For those who wanted them, there was an astonishing variety of theatres where plays were performed in Yiddish. The most famous of the actors was Boris Thomashefsky, who became the romantic idol of the East Side, a plump man who wore his hair long and combed into a pompadour. They said of him that his voice was "made of silk", and no one ever assumed a romantic role with more elegance and impudence. Usually he was to be seen in musical comedies, playing with his wife Bessie, and half the evening they sang duets. There was nothing vulgar in their performances. There was an earthiness about them, but there was also a quality of pure joyfulness. The timid young students of the Talmud, freshly arrived and still wearing earlocks and gabardine, were introduced to an unsuspected aspect of America when they saw the Thomashefskys on the stage. They sang with a gaiety which was curiously American, and they liked to interrupt the flow of Yiddish songs with American patter. The history of the musical comedy stage in America can be traced back to the Thomashefskys, who endowed it with those elements of mockery and impudence and soaring love songs which persist today.

But while the Thomashefskys were the most famous Jewish actors of their time, treated with the dazed respect later shown to film stars, admired, sought after, followed in the streets, drowned in flowers at the end of each opening performance, they had many rivals. The Jewish stage was rich with ancestral colour, and fed from many streams. England, Eastern Europe, and America provided its traditions. *Hamlet* and *King Lear* appeared in Yiddish at the Grand Street Theatre—so sumptuous and so over-ornamented a place with its wine-red curtains and gold inlay on the baroque boxes that it suggested paradise in all its ripeness. They were not translations so much as adaptations. *Der Yiddisher Koenig Lear*, played by Jacob Adler, was a Lear of the Russian steppes, a figure of towering majesty though all his kingly robes were removed from him. He was not a king—kings and czars were anathema. Instead he was represented as a great merchant inhabiting a vast palace, straining against the ingratitude of his daughters with all his remaining strength and delivering long monologues to his faithful servant Shammai. Cordelia became Gordele, played by the extravagantly beautiful Bertha Kalich. Lear raved and wept and cursed the heavens, and sometimes his voice dropped to a harrowing whisper as he accused the fates of laughing at his plight. He had the violence of the winter thunder, and by the final curtain he had reduced his audience to tears. Then once more there was that strange feeling of communion, for everyone was Lear, all had suffered and felt themselves to be wanderers on the steppes.

When the first generation of immigrants spoke of *der heym*, they meant the villages they had been forced to abandon, or the great towns of Russia and Poland, or the ghostly Pales of Settlement. They worked and lived in New York, but their imaginations fed on their memories of places to which they would never return. For them *tsuzammen* was the word of greatest resonance: they clung together by instinct, making their closest friends among those who came from the same *gubernias*, the same villages, the same streets.

There were the samovars with Russian tea, the *gefulte* fish, and the long white Sabbath loaves. There were the long hours of work with the stores open from seven in the morning to midnight, and sometimes later. There was the glow of gaslight and the trolley cars rattling across Manhattan Bridge and the Syrian vendors with black velour hats selling glasses of cherry soda for three cents. It was a warm human life, rich with excitement and desire, and with the heady wine of worship. It was a society which answered men's needs, but it began to die when the second generation came to maturity. Perhaps it began to die when the piano music was being thumped out in the nickelodeons.

2

The Young Gershwin

MOSHE GERSHOVITZ was one of those hapless men who came alone to America during the full tide of immigration, with no settled job to go to. He was a slight man who retained to the end of his life a look of quiet bafflement. The story is told that when he arrived in New York Harbour after making the long journey from St. Petersburg, he rushed to the rail of the ship to see the Statue of Liberty, and his hat blew off. In his hatband he had put the address of the only person he knew in all of New York, a tailor called Greenstein. Without the address he was lost. He had nowhere to go, and almost no money. He slept that night on the Bowery, won thirty cents at a pool game and made inquiries about the tailor. No one seemed to know where the tailor lived. At last someone suggested he might be found in Brownsville, and the next day Moshe Gershovitz made his way by trolley car over the Manhattan Bridge, and by dint of much talking and a great deal of luck he found Greenstein the next morning. He worked for the tailor, established himself in Brownsville and then went in search of the Bruskins, a family he had known well in St. Petersburg.

No one remembers how he found the Bruskins or whether he had expected to see them in New York or why he did not search for them as soon as he came to New York. They had been rich in St. Petersburg, while Moshe was poor, had always been poor. His father, Yakob, was an engineer of artillery in the Czar's army, and being a former soldier, one of the "veterans of Nicholas", he was permitted to reside wherever he chose within the Russian Empire: the laws against the Jews did not apply to him. He appears to have been an excellent engineer, and his design for a new type of gun was highly praised by the Ministry of War. After twenty-five years in the army he retired to a small house outside St. Petersburg; and army pensions in Russia were notoriously small. Moshe had grown up among army officers and could look forward to a long career in the engineers' corps, but he had no taste for study, no desire to enter technical college and no liking for war. The laws against the Jews were becoming increasingly harsh, and when he left St. Petersburg he seems to have known he would never see his father again.

He came from a family which had already lost much of its Jewish character—most of the Jews in the engineers' corps paid lip service to the Orthodox Church. Rootless, with no feeling for orthodox Jewish practice, he was one of those "disinherited ones", who had cut themselves adrift.

Almost his first action when he reached New York was to change his name from Gershovitz to Gershvin. There were good, or at least understandable reasons, for the change of name. For some reason the Russian Jews in New York looked down on the Polish Jews; and young Moshe Gershovitz wanted to have a typically Russian name. By this change of name he was announcing that he belonged to the community of Russian Jews. He also changed Moshe to Morris, perhaps because it was fashionable to have a name which could be easily pronounced by Americans, but it is possible that the change was made to demonstrate his indifference to Jewish tradition.

But though he changed his name, there was no change of character. To the end of his life Morris Gershvin resembled the boy who landed penniless in New York, slight and wiry, with features that were more Polish than Russian, and he was excitable and amusing in a typically Polish way. He shared with his father a passion for tinkering with machines, and he may have derived from his father his lasting admiration for uniforms. Unlike his father, who spent his whole active life in the engineers' corps, Morris Gershvin was one of those shiftless people who change jobs every few months.

He was changing jobs almost as soon as he arrived in New York. For a short while he was employed in the manufacture of the uppers of women's shoes, but he soon resigned. At various times in his life he was a baker, a bookie, a restaurant owner, the manager of a Turkish bath, the owner of a cigar stall and pool parlour on 42nd Street, the landlord of a rooming-house, and the operator of a summer hotel. He liked to be close to his place of work, and he was therefore continually changing his address. It has been calculated that during the period of twenty-two years following his marriage in 1895 he moved nearly thirty times.

Few solemn acts are recorded in his life, but his marriage to Rose Bruskin, the daughter of the gentle red-bearded furrier he had known in St. Petersburg, was one of them. Rose was plump, dark-eyed, and pretty in a Victorian way; and she had inherited from her father a sensible attitude towards money. She was perfectly aware of her husband's faults. His shiftlessness was one of the facts of life, and she could do little to change it, but she could, and did, become the family banker. She superintended the cash receipts and expenditures whenever her husband was managing a restaurant or a hotel. Capital was salted away into diamonds, and when money was urgently needed, the diamonds would be pawned. Married to a man who seemed to change his jobs for entirely capricious reasons, she came in time to regard money as the one stable element in the universe. It was not that she was avaricious. It was simply that she was the daughter of a merchant and attached to money a quite extraordinary virtue.

The Gershvins were never poor, but their early lives were spent amid surroundings of poverty. Sometimes they kept a maid, but maids were cheap, and in any event it would have been impossible for Rose Gershvin to bring up a family while looking after the cash registers without a maid. Outwardly they appeared to be a typically lower middle-class family, and no one ever went hungry for long. They went from one drab apartment or railroad flat to another, and always managed to keep their heads above water.

Their first son, Israel, was born on December 6, 1896. Two years later, on September 26, 1898, their second son, Yacob, was born. He was named after his grandfather, the old retired military engineer who was still living in St. Petersburg. Once more there was a baffling series of name changes. Israel became Isidore, and then Ira. Yacob, for no reason that anyone ever understood, became George. About this time Morris Gershvin changed his name to Gershwin or Gershwine.

So it happened that Moshe Gershovitz became the father of George Gershwin.

As a boy George Gershwin could hardly be distinguished from the thousands of Jewish boys living on the East Side. He went to school, played in the streets, and worshipped the New York Giants. He rarely read a book, skipped school whenever possible, and liked fights. He especially liked roller-skating and street hockey, and was something of a champion in the outdoor sports played in schoolyards and in the shadow of tenements, unlike his brother Ira who developed at an early age an enduring passion for books. George played "cat"; Ira read dime novels. George sauntered up and down the street picking fights, while Ira remained indoors. The brothers in fact showed fundamentally different attitudes towards the world. When George played truant or forgot his homework, it was Ira, two years older, who had to go down to the school and make the proper apologies.

Seeing them in their childhood, one might guess that Ira would become a professor and George a light heavyweight boxer. Inevitably they would go their own way, for neither of the parents had much control over them. It was a family without traditions and without any real adherence to Jewish customs: only Ira was *bar mitzvahed*. The boys lived among Jews, but in effect they were quickly losing their Jewishness, to become almost indistinguishable from the *goyim*, whose traditions and mores they accepted without a qualm.

No one in the family had shown any musical talent. Morris could sing a little, but no one ever suggested that he should take up singing as a profession. George had no ear for music, regarded children who took piano lessons as "sissies", and was supremely bored by the music classes in school, when to the tinkling of the piano the children were encouraged to sing *Annie Laurie* or *The Lost Chord*. The undisputed hockey champion of the street gave it as his opinion that anyone who played a fiddle or sang opera must have something wrong with him. It was not so much that he was bored by music, as that music had no place in his existence.

There were, however, occasional moments when he dimly perceived that music answered some need in him. Long afterward, when the memory of these days had become blurred, he remembered being haunted by the tune of "I'll take the high road and you take the low road", but he could not remember why he preferred this tune to *The Lost Chord*. He remembered being pleased by the jaunty melodies of the Gilbert and Sullivan operettas. There was a more famous occasion when he stood outside a penny arcade listening to an automatic piano leaping through Rubinstein's *Melody in F*. "The peculiar jumps in the music held me rooted," he said. "To this very day I can't hear the tune without picturing myself outside that arcade on 125th Street,

standing there barefoot and in overalls, drinking it all in avidly."
He thought he was six years old when he heard the *Melody in F*.
He remembered it as one might remember a fire which took
place in a neighbouring street. There was excitement and a blaze
of light and then the darkness came down again.

He was growing up very normally. At school he thought he
had a talent for painting, but a teacher exploded with laughter
when he showed her a painting, and many years passed before he
attempted painting again. He was nine when he fell in love for the
first time. The girl, who was his own age, had a pleasant singing
voice, and he wondered afterwards, when he had forgotten her
name, whether it was her voice which attracted him to her. They
were inseparable. They walked hand-in-hand down the street. It
was a bad case of puppy love, but it passed when the girl went to
live elsewhere. He was not unduly perturbed, rejoined the gang,
and became once more the bravo, who feared no one and would
cheerfully fight people twice his size. Stories were told of his
petty thievery, and people whispered that not much good could
be expected from George Gershwin.

The East Side was a forcing ground of all the talents. The
youngsters who grew up in the streets were made keen-witted by
poverty and the drabness of the endless brownstone houses. They
had no traditions, no settled way of life, no well-defined aims.
There were streets where they could walk unhindered, and other
streets where they would be greeted with cries of "sheeny". Then
there were murderous fights, bloody noses, followed by a sudden
descent of the cops, who would nearly always take the part of the
goyim, those fair-haired foreigners who guarded the gates which
led into the outside world.

The East Side was a perilous place, where everyone learned to
fight for survival. Boys who were to become murderers lived
cheek by jowl with boys who were to become famous artists or
owners of great industrial chains, millionaire art patrons, and
leaders of society. The thrust was there. Instinctively they
developed a fiercely competitive spirit, knowing they were
doomed to sweltering anonymity unless they broke through the
barricades. Competition was the drug that kept them from
going insane.

They remembered George Gershwin as one of those who were
dedicated to competition. He was always trying to prove himself,

always trying to show himself superior to his fellows. He was determined to be the best at anything he touched, but no one ever guessed that he would touch music.

The first real encounter with music came at the age of ten, when he was attending Public School 25 at Fifth Street and Second Avenue.

According to the school custom, promising piano and violin students were encouraged to give recitals in the school auditorium after lunch. Compulsory attendance was not demanded, and while some children sat and listened to the music, others played in the school yard. George was kicking a ball in the yard when the sound of Dvořák's *Humoresque* came floating through the window. George stopped kicking the ball and listened, enchanted by the haunting music, which came to him, as he said later, like "a flashing revelation of beauty".

He knew who was playing the violin—the eight-year-old Maxie Rosenzweig, the son of a local barber. Maxie was small and pale, one of those studious boys who took no part in the "sporting set". George barely knew him. Normally he would have regarded it as a disgrace to be seen in Maxie's company. But standing in the school yard, he decided he had never heard anything so accomplished or so beautiful. All that life had ever meant for him and all the promise it held for him seemed to be bound up with that sweet and sinister lament.

He decided to make friends with Maxie, and waited for him to come through the school yard. He played truant, staying in the yard when he should have been attending classes, because he did not want to miss his new friend. He waited from three o'clock until half-past four in the pouring rain, but though other children came out of school, there was no sign of Maxie, who had left through the teachers' entrance.

He was at his wits' end. He had heard the music, and there seemed to be a kind of conspiracy to prevent him from congratulating the violinist. He made inquiries, found out Maxie's address, and then, dripping wet, he went to the boy's house, only to learn that Maxie had left. Disconsolate and close to weeping, George stammered out a request. He wanted them to tell Maxie how much he liked his music.

That was the first of many visits to the Rosenzweig house, for a meeting was arranged and the boys were thereafter inseparable.

Though he was only eight Maxie was George's intellectual superior; he had been studying music since the age of three, and instinctively knew more about the world than George, who became his pupil, his friend and worshipping admirer. From Maxie, George heard the names of Beethoven and Mozart for the first time. They wrote letters to each other, though they lived only a few blocks apart. They wrestled together, and George won. But when they argued intellectually, Maxie always won.

George decided to follow in Maxie's footsteps: he too would become a musician. For fifty cents a lesson he acquired the services of a lady piano teacher. There was a succession of teachers, and none of them found very much merit in the pupil. Even Maxie was not impressed with George's progress. "You haven't got it in you, Georgie," he said. "Take my word for it, I can tell!"

George seems to have felt that the fault lay in the teachers. He despised the anonymous lady pianists and searched for teachers with greater authority who would not force him through the drudgery of playing Beyer's *Exercises*. Authority came in the shape of a musician called Goldfarb, a former leader of a Hungarian band. Goldfarb was a volatile man, hugely impressed by his own importance, expansive and ignorant. He charged $1.50 a lesson and set George to working on excerpts from grand opera. In six months he had advanced as far as the overture to *William Tell* which he played with abandon, if without any grace. It was Goldfarb's theory that one should not pay too much attention to the notes: the important thing was to play *con brio* and with divine excitement. George felt there was something obscurely wrong in these lessons, and searched for a better teacher.

Meanwhile he had acquired a piano of his own. It was originally intended for Ira, who had shown some promise as a musician but failed to complete more than a few pages of Beyer's *Exercises*. Ira was only too glad for an excuse to let George have the piano. The family was surprised to discover that George at the age of twelve was able to play complicated bravura passages, with exaggerated rubatos and quick changes of tempo. He could play *Humoresque* and an endless series of pot-pourri from Italian operas. He played the overture to *William Tell* continually until, as he thought, he had perfected it.

He was thirteen or fourteen when he met Charles Hambitzer and learned that there was something terribly wrong with his playing of the overture. Hambitzer, with his dark deep-sunk eyes and studied gestures, spoke with real authority. His great-grandfather had been court violinist to Czar Nicholas I. He was a composer and piano soloist of considerable fame, and he was still more famous as a teacher of piano, violin and 'cello. It was said that he could play every instrument in the orchestra. When George sat down to play the overture to *William Tell* Hambitzer was full of encouragement. When he finished playing, Hambitzer jumped out of his chair and exclaimed, "Who taught you to play like that? Let's hunt out that guy and shoot him—and not with an apple on his head, either!"

George became the pupil of Hambitzer, and never regretted it. He had found his master, the man who knew so much more about music than anyone he had ever encountered. The new teacher was one of those rare men whose gift for music is only equalled by his understanding of people. Nothing gave him greater pleasure than a pupil who worked hard and joyously. Hambitzer introduced him to Chopin, Liszt, and Debussy; and these were influences that remained.

There were to be many more teachers, but George always pointed to Hambitzer as the one who taught him most and made the greatest impression on him. Once he said, "Without Hambitzer, there would be no Gershwin," and that was true. Maxie Rosenzweig, who was to become a famous violinist under the name of Max Rosen, provided the original spark, but it was Hambitzer, who never achieved much fame and died at thirty-seven, who blew on the spark and made it flame.

George was a good pupil who worked hard and asked intelligent questions. Hambitzer could be strict, but he had the power to bring the best out of his pupils, and he was deeply impressed with George's deadly seriousness. It was Hambitzer, too, who introduced George to the world of symphony concerts, giving him lists of the things he should hear.

In the family it was generally agreed that George's artistic gifts were insufficient to provide him with an income. His skill at mathematics was reasonably good, and it was thought that he might pursue a career as an accountant or a banker. Accordingly, at fourteen, he was sent to a commercial school to learn type-writing, shorthand and double-entry book-keeping. At the worst he could be employed in one of his father's business ventures.

Morris Gershwin liked to say that without discipline and sound training the boy would never amount to anything.

George had other ideas. He hated double-entry book-keeping and he adored music—any kind of music. Hambitzer had written light operas, though he had failed to make any money from them. When George remarked one day that popular music was as much worth composing as classical music, Hambitzer agreed, although his preference lay in the more serious music which he rarely composed. George was beginning to wonder whether he could make a living as a pianist or a composer of songs.

His first composition to be performed publicly was a tango which he played in March 1914 for an entertainment at Christadora House on Avenue B. The entertainment had largely been arranged by Ira for members of a club belonging to the College of the City of New York. The tango occupied the place of honour at the beginning of the performance, and copies of the programme listing "*Piano solo . . . George Gershvin*" are still in existence.

Two months after the performance George abandoned the commercial school. Quite suddenly, with no more than a few days' warning to his family, he became a song-plugger in Tin Pan Alley, at the respectable salary of $15 a week. He was fifteen, and the youngest song-plugger known to the trade.

He was on his own—a tall, well-built boy with brown eyes and hair brushed back straight from the forehead and slicked down, deceptively mild until he sat down at the piano and then he played like an abandoned demon. Sometimes—and this happened especially when he was being photographed—his features would shape themselves into a look of profound melancholy, but the melancholy melted before the piano. He had a powerful touch, and his arms were like a boxer's. His family was almost hysterical when he gave up book-keeping, but most of those who knew him thought he would make his way.

He was still untried, with very little musical knowledge, and most of it he had derived during the brief months he had studied under Hambitzer. For the rest he had found music in the air as he wandered about the streets of the East Side. He had heard much Jewish folk music, seen many musical comedies in the Jewish theatres, and listened to those strange glassed-in machines in the nickel arcades which permitted you to hear two minutes of music through earplugs, and he had attended perhaps twenty concerts.

One influence above all was to dominate him, though he was perhaps unaware of it—the influence of Jewish traditional music.

Recently Carl Van Vechten, who knew him better than most people, declared, "It's absurd to talk about Jewish tradition in George Gershwin. There was nothing notably Jewish in him at all. Why, we never thought of it!"

Yet he was a Jew, and grew up steeped in that magnificent and troubled heritage. Again and again we shall come upon evidence of that influence, which was perhaps all the greater because he never gave it a thought.

3

Tin Pan Alley

TIN PAN ALLEY was a clutter of brownstone houses on 28th Street, just off Fifth Avenue, only a few blocks from the seething garment district and a stone's throw from Pennsylvania Station. Even in those days it was a drab street with no pretensions to elegance, though the dreams of the nation were manufactured there. Here songs were merchandised, packaged, and distributed. Fortunes were made by young men picking out new melodies on tinny pianos. It was the time when nearly every house had a piano in the parlour and sheet music sold in the hundreds of thousands of copies.

No one remembers how Tin Pan Alley got its name, just as no one remembers the origin of the words "jazz" or "blues"; and no one cares. The names were right. They suggested exactly the right mingling of sound and fury. In Tin Pan Alley the pianos were pounded all day, and all day there was a stream of producers, singers, actors, and orchestra leaders searching for hits. They went into the cage-like cubicles, listened to the sales talk and the high-pressure patter of the pianist who would sing the song while playing and interrupt himself to enlarge on the inevitable success of the song once it had been bought by the customer. Sales resistance was strong. There were perhaps a hundred song-pluggers in the street, and more than enough songs to choose from. Every day a deafening orgy of sound rose from the embattled street. Tap dancers danced, instrumentalists rehearsed, bands played, the song-pluggers shouted. It was the time before soundproof walls, and before radio and phonographs. Jazz had just been born, and Tin Pan Alley was at the height of its power.

The power of Tin Pan Alley extended wherever songs were sung. It was big business, and pathetically competitive and ruthless. There were all the vices of competition—payola, outright bribery, fraud, contempt for the audience. Every new device was exploited. When the nickelodeons were still in the chrysalis stage, and there was no soundtrack on the films, Tin Pan Alley arranged that during the intervals slides with the words of popular songs should be flashed on the screens, and the songs were taken up and sung by people planted in the audience. These, too, were song-pluggers.

The song-pluggers were everywhere. They went to the vaudeville houses, applauding their own songs vociferously and making sure that the audience also applauded. They were always buttonholing singers. They travelled with vaudeville companies. They formed the selling arm of mass entertainment at a time when mass entertainment was largely restricted to theatres and vaudeville houses.

Gershwin was a good song-plugger. He had strong hands and could pound out songs all day and all night, never tiring. Every morning at nine o'clock he entered his cubicle and played popular tunes for anyone who cared to listen. Years later he remembered how coloured people came and asked him to play "God Send You Back To Me" in seven keys. He remembered chorus girls breathing down his neck, but most of all he remembered the customers who blew cigar smoke into his face and asked him to play and then after a few bars dismissed the song with biting comments. "Some of them treated me like dirt," he said. And he remembered the feeling that came over him when he realized that song-plugging had no future for him. He would grow old, pounding out other people's rubbish, and never get anywhere. There was fifteen dollars a week, and small commissions if he succeeded in selling a song, and that was all.

He was not bitter. Most of the time he enjoyed the job, developing his remarkable facility. By good fortune he entered Tin Pan Alley just at the time when jazz was beginning to be the rage, having accomplished its long journey from the levees of New Orleans to New York. Jazz was hot music, with a wild beat that immediately appealed to him; and even in the worst jazz there was little of the deadening monotony of the songs he was forced to play. Most wearying of all were the evenings when he went out with a corps of song-pluggers accompanied by a song-and-dance team, and then the hit songs would be pounded out in the New York cafés.

Still, there were advantages in song-plugging. He was learning to know the business of popular music. He was travelling a little, following a group of vaudeville actors across New Jersey. He had spent part of the summer of 1912 playing the piano in a hotel in the Catskills—this was his first recorded excursion outside the city of New York. But travel, though it broadened him, did not appeal to him. He belonged to New York.

He was learning all the time and developing new admirations. He especially admired Irving Berlin and Jerome Kern. Irving Berlin had started the hard way, as a song-plugger at Tony Pastor's Music Hall on Union Square. He had been a singing waiter in the Bowery. He had written lyrics and sold them for a few cents and been grateful. By 1909, when he wrote "Sadie Salome Go Home", he was famous, and he became still more famous two years later when he wrote "Alexander's Ragtime Band", which was played across the nation and wherever American songs were sung. Irving Berlin became the "King of Ragtime". He went on to write complete scores for musical operas. In 1913, when Gershwin entered Tin Pan Alley, it was a name which men spoke with bated breath. Years later Gershwin would say of him that he was the greatest of all American song composers—"our Franz Schubert".

Irving Berlin lived on the starry heights; Jerome Kern was a less intimidating figure. When Gershwin's Aunt Kate was married in 1914, the band had played Kern's "You're Here and I'm Here" from *The Girl From Utah*, and Gershwin was so excited by the music that he dashed over to the band-leader and asked the name of the piece. Thereafter he was always looking out for Kern's music, studying its melodic line and trying to discover the secret of its success. He paid Kern the tribute of imitation and wrote a number of songs which were wholly imitative. From Kern he learned that musical comedy music could be a vast improvement on the popular songs he pounded out in his cubicle. Already he began to see himself as a composer of musical comedies.

He was restless, straining every nerve and getting nowhere.

He was growing weary of being a hired hack, and there was some puritan element in him which rebelled against the morals of Tin Pan Alley. He disliked, too, the loud vulgarity and gaudy clothes of the other song-pluggers. There was only one way out —the way of Irving Berlin and Jerome Kern. More than ever he wanted to write songs, but when he showed a song he had written to his employer, he was told, "We want you as a pianist, not as a composer." In desperation he showed the songs to Irving Berlin who advised him to keep on writing, seeing much promise in them but very little fulfilment.

One day while he was still eagerly seeking a way out of song-plugging, there came an extraordinary invitation from Boris Thomashefsky, the great actor and impresario who ran the National Theatre. Thomashefsky had lost the services of his composer, Joseph Rumshinsky, who had composed the music for innumerable operettas and maintained the musical tradition of the still more famous Abraham Goldfaden. Rumshinsky had left Thomashefsky's theatre to take over the musical direction of the Second Avenue Theatre. The gap had to be filled quickly, but how?

Thomashefsky was in a quandary, until it suddenly occurred to him that there was a brilliant solution to the problem. He turned to two young musicians he knew well.

The first was Sholom Secunda, who had only recently graduated from Juilliard. Secunda was shy, scholarly and deeply versed in orthodox music, and could be relied upon to provide a brilliant knowledge of orchestration. George Gershwin was something else altogether. He was "the wild one", the man who could improvise brilliantly and endlessly, the tyro who attacked music as a matador will attack a bull. In spite of the lessons he was receiving from Hambitzer, Gershwin still had difficulty reading music, and in fact he was not interested in reading music. He played by ear. Thomashefsky had come to the conclusion that Secunda plus Gershwin equals Rumshinsky.

There were many reasons why Thomashefsky should have thought of Gershwin. Gershwin was a friend of the family and a constant visitor to the National Theatre. He had attended the operettas night after night, soaking up the atmosphere of the theatre. He ran errands for the actors. He had appeared on stage in crowd scenes. Almost he was a part of the theatre, and a good deal of his musical knowledge had been derived from listening to Joseph Rumshinsky's scores. For a while Boris Thomashefsky's son Harry had been Gershwin's closest friend. There are many people still living who can remember Rose Gershwin playing cards night after night with the actresses in the theatre. The entire

Gershwin family were *habitués* of the theatre, and they were never asked to pay.

On that Saturday afternoon Secunda and Gershwin sat in Thomashefsky's dressing-room, playing to one another and discussing the extraordinary offer which had been made to them. Gershwin admitted that he had only the most rudimentary knowledge. He was paralysed by fright. He said he was not a musician in any real sense. He was a song-plugger, and he was not at all sure he could play the music Thomashefsky demanded because his techniques, such as they were, were adapted to Tin Pan Alley. He wanted to write for the Jewish theatre where he could be assured of a reasonable salary and a forty-week contract, but he was troubled by Secunda's academic proficiency, and Secunda in turn was troubled by Gershwin's vast ignorance. In the end it was Secunda who backed out of the arrangement.

Recently Secunda has been wondering what would have happened if Gershwin had remained with the Jewish theatre. He feels that Gershwin was admirably equipped to compose music for the theatre, though he would have needed more training. "If it had not been for my stubborn judgement," he said recently, "I feel he would have remained with Thomashefsky. In my opinion the Jewish theatre lost more than he did as a result of my stubbornness."

In fact Gershwin never did depart very far from the Jewish theatre. The influence of Goldfaden and Rumshinsky remained with him to the end; and behind the figure of Gershwin there can be discerned the large and imposing figure of Thomashefsky, plump and beatific, crowding the stage with those endless improvisations in which he appeared now as a character from the Bible, now as one of the heroes of the Chassidic movement, leaping and dancing, summoning God to look down on the sufferings of the Jews, and all this in a theatre given over to musical comedy: musical, but not always comic.

For whatever else he was Gershwin was a child of his times, and it was beyond his power to avoid the influences which dominated his youth. The strength of his music came from the strange marriage of Jewish musical comedy and jazz, and from that improvident *chutzpah* which he always regarded as his greatest virtue and his greatest vice.

But that quality of *chutzpah*, which can best be translated as

George Gershwin

Gershwin at the piano surrounded by theatrical celebrities. Left to right: Jack Donohue, Marilyn Miller, George Gershwin, Sigmund Romberg and Florenz Ziegfeld

Distributed by United Artists Associated Incorporated

Scene from the Warner Brothers' film *Rhapsody in Blue*

"sheer effrontery", was not yet in evidence during the days he was song-plugging. Outwardly he showed a devil-may-care attitude; inwardly he was a very frightened young man waiting for a break, and there was no break in sight. He was still composing songs in his spare time. He was still trying to attract the attention of Jerome Kern and spent long hours standing outside his window, hoping to meet the great man or to hear him play. He was still getting nowhere.

He was seventeen when his first song was published. It was not by any means a good song and showed none of the promise he was to show a few years later. It was called "When You Want 'Em You Can't Get 'Em", and for this he received five dollars from Harry von Tilzer. Gershwin wrote the music. The lyrics were written by Murray Roth, who received fifteen dollars.

This, however, was a beginning, and soon there was a spate of songs which he touted from one publisher to another without success. With Murray Roth he wrote another song, "My Runaway Girl", which pleased Sigmund Romberg, who invited him to bring more songs, but there was no sudden leap into fame. To make money he cut a few piano rolls and took on odd jobs. Song-plugging was becoming unbearable, and he gave it up in March 1917 and spent the summer at a series of aimless jobs. He wanted to study, he hankered after musical respectability and he was still feeling his way. He took up the saxophone, and learned to play it reasonably well, and he tried to sell his songs. He played in a Brooklyn night-club. He became a rehearsal pianist in the Century Theatre just off Union Square for thirty-five dollars a week, a more princely sum than any he had received up to this time. Rehearsals bored him, and he amused himself by subtle improvisations. The Century Theatre was preparing to put on *Miss 1917*, one more of the endless musical comedies which were doomed to failure, but there were advantages in pounding the piano and watching the dancers go through their paces. The theatre was his appointed home and he was beginning to meet some of the successful promoters and singers. In the course of a few days he met Jerome Kern, Victor Herbert, P. G. Wodehouse, Lew Fields, and Vivienne Segal. And when the rehearsals were over, he became the accompanist of the singers who performed in the Sunday evening concerts. At one of these concerts in November, two of his songs were sung by Vivienne

Segal, and then at last he began to feel that he was making headway.

The song-plugging was over, but the hack work went on. He was playing the piano wherever he could be heard. He was still trying to sell his songs—there were already drawers full of them—and he was still trying to force his way into musical comedy. But the only job he succeeded in landing was that of accompanist to Louise Dresser as she sang her way through the Keith vaudeville circuit. It was beginning to look as though the first glimpse of fame provided by the Century Theatre when he took his bows with Vivienne Segal was a will-o'-the-wisp. He was in danger of becoming the eternal accompanist, travelling across the country in the tow of some famous singer. What he wanted was time to develop, and time was the one thing he could not afford.

Time, leisure, opportunity to study came suddenly and unexpectedly when he was invited to call on Max Dreyfus, who had been the first to detect the promise of Jerome Kern. Dreyfus was the head of the Harms publishing house, a cautious wily man not given to sudden enthusiasms, quiet and reserved. He rarely showed emotion, and he showed none to Gershwin. He simply made an offer—Gershwin could draw up to thirty-five dollars a week as long as he wrote music and presented it to the Harms company. He was provided with a cubicle and a piano. There were no fixed hours, no fixed duties. For the next twelve years all Gershwin's music was published by Dreyfus. The investment paid off handsomely.

It was a stroke of luck, but the luck was deserved. Gershwin had been attempting to break into show business with all his strength and all his resources, with never a moment of the day when he was not thinking about advancing himself. It had not been easy. Appearances were against him. He looked like a young rabbi. He was rather swarthy, and there was a curious reserve about him, which attracted some and offended others. He was now a salaried composer, and in his spare time he could still take on odd jobs to supplement his income.

Among the jobs he took on was accompanist to Nora Bayes, a vaudeville singer then widely known, starring in a show called *Ladies First*. Gershwin was hired for a six-weeks tour, which brought him to Pittsburgh, where Oscar Levant, a boy in knee breeches, grew tired of the singer and found himself watching the pianist with mounting admiration. He remembered later that he had never heard "such a brisk, unstudied, completely free and inventive playing, all within a consistent framework". Later Oscar Levant was to become Gershwin's most devoted and sardonic admirer.

Gershwin's relations with Nora Bayes were turbulent. She was always criticizing him, and she knew all his weakest points, for she too had been brought up on the Lower East Side. He did not like the way she sang his songs, and she found fault with his music. Once she asked him to change the ending of a song. He refused. She reminded him that famous composers had bowed to her will.

"Irving Berlin and Jerome Kern always change songs for me when I ask them," she said.

"I put a lot of work in that song," Gershwin replied testily, "and I am not going to change it for anyone. You'll have to sing it as it is!"

Nora Bayes raged, but Gershwin remained adamant. He was still unsure of himself and would usually change a song immediately if anyone so much as suggested the slightest change, but he was weary of her tantrums, and most of all he was weary of her singing. More than ever he was determined to abandon accompanying. What he wanted to do was to write an entire show. Jerome Kern had warned him that he was not yet ready for it, but he was beginning to believe he had acquired the experience and the knowledge to do almost anything he pleased on the musical comedy stage.

For Nora Bayes he had written the song "Some Wonderful Sort of Someone". Gershwin put great hopes on the song, but when Nora Bayes sang it, there was only polite applause. Later it was put into a show called *Lady in Red*, and brought down the house. More and more his songs were to be found in musical comedies on Broadway: sometimes single songs, often two or three songs, rarely more.

The opportunity to write a whole show came one day when he was working in his cubicle at Harms, and Dreyfus was talking to a promoter called Perkins who wanted to write a show around Joe Cook, the comedian famous for his inconsequential patter about four Hawaiians. Perkins was in a quandary. He wanted the music quickly. There was to be music for an orchestra of twenty-five coloured musicians, Joe Cook, a bicycle act, and a Broadway chorus. But when the show opened in Syracuse, N.Y. the chorus had melted away, and the cast had to improvise a chorus as best they could, wearing Chinese hats which covered their faces, jiggling and dancing beneath the hats while pretending to be chorus girls.

The show was called *Half-past Eight*, and this was a misnomer, for the curtain rose much later. There was trouble from the beginning. The first-night seats had been bought out by an organization which immediately regretted its folly. The performers suspected rightly that they would not receive their pay envelopes, and by the Wednesday following the Monday opening they were in a state of mutiny. One group of performers refused to go on, and Gershwin, dressed in a blue suit and unshaven, was ordered on to the stage.

"What do I do?" he asked.

"Play some of your songs," he was told. "Keep 'em amused."

Gershwin had never refused to play his songs in public, and obediently went on. He played a medley of his songs, some of them already famous, but the audience with their eyes on the programmes wondered what it was all about. There was no applause when he left the stage. The reviewers unanimously damned the show. *Variety* wrote: $2 *Show Not Worth War Tax*.

Half-past Eight was a failure, but Gershwin had learned his lesson. In future there were no more speculative shows produced by inexperienced producers with inadequate backing. There were to be failures again, many of them, but never a failure as exhausting and silly as this one. After *Half-past Eight*, whenever there were failures, Gershwin could blame only himself.

Alex Aarons was the son of a rich clothing manufacturer with a long musical tradition in his family. He composed a little, and his father was always composing. He had daring and knowledge, and he was still young enough—he was under thirty—to have a feeling for the musical taste of the men who were coming back from the war. He wanted the new, the exciting, the dissonant. He wanted catchy songs which would suddenly take off in unexpected directions, and for some time he had had his eyes on Gershwin, who was invited to write a new musical comedy to be called *La La Lucille*. It was his first full musical comedy score. It was light, dexterous, frothy. Brooks Atkinson, writing for the *Boston Even-*

ing Transcript, said it was vivacious and full of surprising details and harmoniously pleasing. Some of the songs were cannibalized from the unfortunate *Half-past Eight*; others were taken from the drawer; but most of them were written for the show itself. The story had something to do with a dentist who was left two million dollars by his aunt on condition that he divorce his wife Lucille, a chorus girl who for some reason had incurred the aunt's displeasure. The plot was as inconsequential as Joe Cook's famous monologues, but Gershwin had proved that he could write the music for a full-length musical. He was to write twenty-seven more in a period of eighteen years; of these only four were failures.

La La Lucille opened at the Henry Miller Theatre in May 1919 and played throughout the summer to a total of 104 performances. It was a moderate hit, proving only that Gershwin was a good craftsman. There was no fire from heaven, and the Hudson River did not burst into flame. But in the same year he wrote the first of the songs which were to bring his name to the attention of millions.

"Swanee" was born one evening during a bus ride along Riverside Drive. He had been dining with Irving Caesar at Dinty Moore's restaurant and they had tossed ideas to one another about a one-step somewhat in the style of "Hindustan". Caesar suggested there were advantages in avoiding an Indian background. "Keep it to America," he said, and murmured something about the Deep South. They talked for a while about Stephen Foster, and gradually the pattern of the song arose, compounded out of the rhythm of the bus, Offenbach's *Barcarolle*, and Stephen Foster. There never was a song which owed so much to so many ancestors, but though the melodic line can be traced to many sources, it existed in its own right as a pleasing melody. The song had already taken shape in their minds when they reached the Washington Heights section of New York, where Gershwin was then living. Gershwin sat down at the piano and played the tune, while poker players behind the beaded curtain which separated the piano room from the living-room shouted at the composer and the librettist, and soon Morris Gershwin was playing the tune through a piece of tissue paper and a comb. The poker players stopped playing and crowded round the piano, and they were all singing it. They were present at the birth of a song which was to sweep the world.

"Swanee" is a strange hybrid, like so many of Gershwin's songs. Isaac Goldberg said it was born "right in Our Alley, by pseudo-Dixie out of Judæo-Gypsy Land", but it was in fact more Judæo than Gypsy, and Dixie was so pseudo that it had lost all meaning. "Swanee" marked an end to the long tradition of southern folksong with a residue of meaning. "Swanee" was nonsense verse of quite extraordinary banality, to a tune of quite extraordinary enchantment; and no one, once he had heard it, would ever forget it.

Surprisingly, "Swanee" was a failure when it was first performed in a band arrangement at the Capitol Theatre. No one left the theatre humming the tune, and no newspapers announced that a superlative tune had come into existence. Max Dreyfus admired it; Irving Caesar offered to sell his rights in it for two hundred dollars; Gershwin was puzzled by the failure. Some months later Al Jolson gave a party and Gershwin played the piano and sang some of his songs. He sang "Swanee", and Jolson was enraptured. He wanted the song for his forthcoming production of *Sinbad* at the Winter Garden, where he sang it to tumultuous applause, and sixty chorus girls with electric lights in their shoes sang the chorus. Then "Swanee" was accepted as a classical hit, and soon everyone in America was singing it. In a year more than a million copies of the sheet music were sold. Its fame reached as far as Constantinople, where the young musician Vernon Duke heard it and was enchanted by it, when he was earning a precarious living playing the piano at a night spot called the *Mayak*. What delighted him most of all, as he wrote later, was "the bold sweep of the tune, its rhythmic freshness and especially its syncopated gait", and he noted that the name of the composer was improbably spelled "Geo. Gershwin". He had not heard of Gershwin before, but he resolved that if ever he came to America he would call on the composer, who seemed to have all the sophistication in the world at his fingertips.

"Swanee" is still sung, and threatens to outlast all Gershwin's songs. More than most of his songs it has the quality of *memorability*. It is a hodge-podge, just as "Yes, We Have No Bananas" is a hodge-podge derived from Handel's *Messiah* and half a dozen other sources, but it bears the characteristic sign-manual of Gershwin—his weariness, his gaiety, his use of jazzed-up Jewish melodies mingling with melodies derived at a distance from

American tradition. Somewhere below the surface of nearly all the music he ever wrote can be discerned a plaintive lament or a Jewish lullaby.

So it was, too, with most of the composers who came out of Tin Pan Alley—those exiles in a foreign land who dreamed of a warm South and a warm and beckoning Mammy, "who is waiting and praying for me." Swanee and Dixie were interchangeable and without meaning, but the hunger was real. They thrived on their dreams of imaginary Dixies, but to the end they remained Jews, improvising on Jewish themes, being all the more Jewish because they had abandoned their heritage and were hardly aware that the heritage existed. Because they were empty of traditions, tradition poured through them. Swanee was only another name for the remote villages of Russia and Poland which still summoned them, or perhaps it was another name for Jerusalem.

4

Rhapsody in Blue

OUTWARDLY Gershwin gave the impression of a man moving forward by sudden jerky leaps. He belonged to the age of jazz, the Charleston, the Black Bottom, the break in the rhythm, the throbbing wounds of the war he never fought and the South he had never seen. He was Horatio Alger with a fur-lined collar and dancing hands. He was the man who had pushed ahead to become at twenty-one almost as famous as his heroes, Irving Berlin and Jerome Kern. He could always be relied upon to provide a tune, and inevitably he would gravitate towards Broadway, the big lights, the "shmaltzy" musical comedies, the plush apartment on Riverside Drive, and the soaring bank balance.

This was the pattern, and he came dangerously close to following it. Having no innate culture of his own, he must adapt himself to the culture around him, assuming like a chameleon the colours of the world around him. Having no fixed goals, he must let himself be carried by the prevailing winds. No one doubted that he would be successful, but many wondered whether he would be remembered. Who remembers the names of the composers of musical comedies written fifty years ago?

Inwardly there were doubts, hesitations, strange interludes of sobriety when he faced his growing fame and wondered whether it could have any meaning. Why was "Swanee" a failure one day, and a shattering success the next? One week he was receiving thirty-five dollars from Max Dreyfus, and the next week there was ten thousand dollars in the bank from the sale of phonograph records and music sheets. Why? He had to ask himself these questions, if only because it was inconceivable to him that his success was unmerited. Most men when they are touched with fame keep wondering why, however brazenly they accept it. Gershwin was no exception: he wondered, and came to a few saving conclusions.

Among those conclusions was an acknowledgement of his own

insufficiency and ignorance. He knew his trade, but knew too little about music. He was determined to learn and was always taking lessons, though he was a restless pupil; and he half-despised the Broadway composers who picked out tunes with one finger and then acquired the services of a tame composer to put the notes on the page. He told himself that in time he would master all the resources of his craft. From his grandfather, if not from his father, he had inherited the habit of study.

So it happened that while one half of him lived in the glare of the footlights, the other half attended to lessons, exercises, classical concerts. Charles Hambitzer was dead—he had killed himself in a fit of despondency in Central Park in 1918, having suffered a few months previously the death of his wife from tuberculosis. More than anyone else he had been able to curb Gershwin's tendency towards easy success. Hambitzer had made a living playing the piano in the Waldorf-Astoria orchestra; his close friend Edward Kilenyi was the violinist in the same orchestra. Kilenyi became Gershwin's teacher. For nearly five years the pupil worked regularly with the teacher, sometimes taking two piano lessons a week, advancing from basic fundamentals to composition, transposition, and instrumentation. Kilenyi was a thorough musician, and drove his pupil hard. He could be caustic when, as sometimes happened, the pupil thought he knew more than he knew, and he could be kindly and amusing when the pupil worked well. On one occasion Kilenyi hired the members of a symphony orchestra one by one to demonstrate to the pupil the possibilities of each separate instrument in the orchestra. Unlike Hambitzer, Kilenyi saw no harm in musical comedies. In his view Gershwin was capable of reaching out in any direction he pleased.

In spite of his growing knowledge Gershwin was too deeply involved in musical comedies to leave them. He was especially attracted by George White's *Scandals*, which were modelled on the *Ziegfeld Follies*. With astonishing audacity George White, a twenty-nine-year-old Canadian, had hoped to topple Ziegfeld from his throne with his *Scandals of 1919* at the Liberty Theatre, taking the leading part himself. Ziegfeld was sufficiently impressed by White to offer him three thousand dollars a week to come over to the *Ziegfeld Follies*; White made a counter-offer offer to Ziegfeld to join the *Scandals* at seven thousand dollars a week. Nothing came of these offers, and *Scandals of 1919* was far from being a critical success.

For *Scandals of 1920* White decided to employ Gershwin as a composer. As an actor White had performed in the ill-fated *Miss 1917* where Gershwin had been the rehearsal pianist; he had been impressed by *La La Lucille*; and he was prepared to give free scope to the composer. For five years Gershwin wrote all the music for the *Scandals*. These compositions added little to his fame, but they gave him financial security, and once, but very briefly, he was permitted to experiment with opera.

It was a very short opera, lasting only twenty minutes, and it appeared for one night only at the opening performance of *Scandals of 1922* on August 29, 1922. It was called *Blue Monday* and described the triangular love affair of Vi, Joe, and Tom. They were Negroes, and the scene was a basement café near 135th Street and Lenox Avenue. Joe was Vi's lover. He leaves New York to see his Mammy in the South, after singing the spiritual, "I'm Going to See my Mother." Vi is not alarmed. It is perfectly natural that Joe should go to the South, but he is away for a long time and Tom, an entertainer in the café, whispers in her ear that perhaps Joe is with another woman. Vi sings her great lament, "Has Anyone Seen my Joe?" When Joe returns, she is sure he "has done her bad", and shoots him. And that is all. The little opera, written in six days, is only barely sustained by the score. The unimpressive libretto by Buddy De Sylva did not help matters. George White decided to remove the opera after opening night. He liked it, but he felt that the introduction of unadulterated violence and melancholy had no place in *Scandals*.

The critics showed no enthusiasm. The theatre critic of the *World* described it as "the most stupid and incredible blackface sketch that has probably ever been presented". Others noted that it was remarkably well-sung and acted, but derived too obviously from *La Bohème* and the *Liebstod* from *Tristan und Isolde*. It was not the overwhelming success Gershwin had hoped for.

Blue Monday is important because it showed the way Gershwin's mind was working. Here in embryo was *Porgy and Bess*. Here, too, was jazz music applied to operatic themes without any attempt to conceal jazz origins. At this time he was talking constantly about writing an opera, and he continued at odd moments to search for a libretto which would satisfy his desire to produce a sustained operatic piece.

Among those who saw *Monday Blues* were Paul Whiteman, "the King of Jazz", who was conducting the orchestra at the *Scandals*, and his arranger, Ferde Grofe, a brilliant composer in his own right. Ferde Grofe's real name was Ferdinand Rudolph von Grofe, but he had long since abandoned his aristocratic connections. He was six years older than Gershwin, and he was to exercise on Gershwin a quite extraordinary influence. The least self-seeking of men, he rarely permitted himself to say he had any influence on Gershwin at all.

All over New York people were talking about Gershwin. This was a reasonably common phenomenon, but there was more than the usual reason for paying attention to him in 1923. His interpolated songs were appearing in many revues and musical comedies, and already a certain beat, a sweetening and quickening of the rhythm, could be detected in his songs. "Swanee" belonged in a class by itself, but "I'll Build a Stairway to Paradise" and "Innocent Ingenue Baby" were pure Gershwin. Both could be traced back to Jewish melodies, but no one was particularly interested in tracing their origins. What was important was that they sounded a new note of amorous triumph and lamentation. They were recognizably his, and people were beginning to comment on his freshness and originality. His fame was reaching beyond Broadway and Tin Pan Alley.

Perhaps the first to recognize the coming of a new and forceful talent which would inevitably influence American music was Carl Van Vechten, a profoundly serious student of American mores who concealed his acute intelligence under the mask of a relentless *bon viveur* and party-goer. Born in Cedar Rapids, he was the provincial who embraces the big town with the fervour of a convert. In his books and essays he showed himself a master of the clever epigram. He liked everything that was new. He was wealthy and self-indulgent and very wise. He was telling everyone, "Watch Gershwin. That young fellow is going to amount to something one day."

Carl Van Vechten was not, of course, alone in seeing Gershwin's potentialities as a serious musician. Many were speaking about him, but few spoke with the authority of Beryl Rubinstein, the concert pianist, who was deeply impressed by Gershwin's inventiveness. "This young fellow has a spark of musical genius," Beryl Rubinstein said. "He has a certain style and seriousness which removes him from the popular-music school altogether, and he must be regarded as one of the really outstanding talents in American musical tradition." George Seldes attempted to define Gershwin's talent, and he found it to be in a certain dreamlike delicacy and in his use of broken rhythms. He wrote in the magazine *The Dial* in August 1923, "Delicacy, even dreaminess, is a quality he alone brings into jazz music. And his sense of variation in rhythm, of an oddly-placed accent, of emphasis and colour, is impeccable."

Concert singers, too, were beginning to pay attention to Gershwin's music. Three months after Gilbert Seldes celebrated Gershwin in the columns of *The Dial*, Eva Gauthier gave a recital at the Aeolian Hall in which she sang her way through a vast programme of songs, including the most ancient and the most modern; and most of the modern songs were written by Gershwin.

Eva Gauthier's appearances were rare and always well-attended. She had a rich voice with an extraordinary range, and on the stage, wearing a black dress and enormous diamond ear-rings, she looked like a *diva*. Her programme was an intimidating one, beginning with Bellini and Purcell, and passing on to Schoenberg, Milhaud, Bartok, and Hindemith. There followed a group of six modern American songs, including one each by Irving Berlin, Jerome Kern, and Walter Donaldson. There followed three by Gershwin—"I'll Build a Stairway to Paradise," "Innocent Ingenue Baby," and "Swanee". Gershwin himself was the accompanist for all the American songs.

He was nervous when he went out on to the stage, a tall slight figure clutching under his arm a bundle of sheet music which in the fashion of the day bore lurid black and yellow covers. He began to play, and at once it became evident that Gershwin was delighting in the rôle of concert pianist, and he was deliberately introducing cross-rhythms and minor variations on the themes. At one point, while playing "I'll Build a Stairway to Paradise" he introduced a brief flourish from Rimsky-Korsakov's *Scheherazade*, which did not pass unnoticed.

Gershwin had stolen the show, demonstrating that jazz had its place on the concert stage. Two days later Deems Taylor was writing in the music section of the Sunday *World*:

It seemed to one listener that the six jazz numbers stood up amazingly well, not only as entertainment but as music. Some of them had their vulgar moments—but it is not for a reviewer who hears the *Marche Slav* and the *Fourteenth Rhapsody* a dozen times a season to open the subject of vulgarity. They are not weighty, but neither is *Lauf der Welt*. They conveyed no profound message—but neither does a good deal of *Also sprach Zarathustra*; at least, they do not pretend to, as Zarathustra does. What they did possess was melodic interest and continuity, harmonic appropriateness, well-balanced, almost classically severe form, and subtle and fascinating rhythms—in short, the qualities that any sincere and interesting music possesses.

The chorus of applause established Gershwin as a composer and pianist of a peculiarly American kind, jaunty, joyous, with the keenest ear for the appropriate musical phrase to reflect his times. The serious critics respected him, and curiously he had little respect for them. He was soon off again on another skirmish with musical comedy: this time it was called *Sweet Little Devil*, with lyrics by Buddy De Sylva. It had its tryout in Boston and was brought to New York, where it played for 120 performances, and was then forgotten. None of the songs belong to the repertoire of Gershwin's successes. *Sweet Little Devil* was done in haste, and Gershwin had no illusions about its lasting value. He was still writing it when he began the most famous and perhaps the most enduring of all his works.

In those days Paul Whiteman was still "the King of Jazz", with no rivals in sight. Starting out from Santa Barbara in California, he had conquered successively Los Angeles, Atlantic City and New York. He had a million dollar income. He controlled eleven bands in New York, seventeen on the road, and received royalties from forty more bands which played his arrangements. In New York he was established in the Palais Royal Nightclub, but he was visibly present in other places—he played on special occasions at hotels, at marriages, at weddings, for George White's *Scandals* and for phonograph companies. In the spring of 1923 he made a triumphal progress through Europe, and returned to America more famous than ever.

It was Paul Whiteman's belief that jazz deserved to be elevated to the stature of great music. "Jazz," he declared, "is the music of our time, and we are not living in an age of decadence. Jazz is the voice of our age." He was not the first to make such claims, but he was the first who could afford to assemble a complete orchestra in a public hall, train his musicians and provide a complete programme of jazz for the delectation of music-lovers. Towards the end of 1923 he was already planning his programme. He discussed it with Gershwin and received the half-promise of a composition of some length on a jazz theme.

Gershwin was so busy with *Sweet Little Devil* that he paid little attention to Whiteman's plans until one day early in January 1924 when he read an announcement in the *New York Tribune*, saying that he was at work on a jazz concerto for Whiteman. The report added that Irving Berlin was writing a syncopated tone poem and Victor Herbert was busy composing an American suite. The programme, designed to answer the question, "What is American music?" was scheduled to take place at Aeolian Hall during the afternoon of February 12, in the presence of Serge Rachmaninoff, Jascha Heifetz, and Efrem Zimbalist. Gershwin had little more than a month in which to compose the concerto, have it orchestrated and rehearsed.

Gershwin called Whiteman on the telephone. What puzzled him more than anything else was the date—February 12th. Whiteman explained that someone else was thinking of putting on a similar programme later in the same month. It was necessary to advance the programme at Aeolian Hall.

"Will you do it, George?" Whiteman asked.

"Yes, but I'll need Ferde Grofe to orchestrate it," Gershwin replied. "I won't have time to do the orchestration, even if I was sure I could orchestrate it properly. I'll write it as a piano concerto."

"That's how I want it," Whiteman said. "Let me know as soon as you are ready."

Gershwin worked best under pressure. He possessed supreme self-assurance. He went to work at once, assembling and discarding ideas for a "blues" concerto, but for some reason none of the thematic material he had accumulated pleased him. He was in love with Liszt's *Second Hungarian Rhapsody*, and the rhapsodic form appealed to him. Gradually there emerged a general theme, very shapeless and diffuse, rhapsodic in nature, beginning nowhere and ending nowhere. He was on the train journeying to

Boston for the premiere of *Sweet Little Devil* when the concerto for the first time came into focus. The train whistles, the rattle of the wheels, the strange symphonic sounds which even the unmusical can hear in the confused roar of a train as it moves rapidly —all these things excited him, until by the time he reached Boston, the complete construction of the rhapsody was present in his mind. The *Rhapsody in Blue* is many things, but it includes the description of a train journey as its central element.

The train journey supplied the beginning and the end. The middle section came into focus a week later when he returned to New York and found himself improvising at a party. "When I am in my normal mood," he said once, "music drips from my fingers." He was in a normal mood at the party. One theme after another dripped from his fingers, but suddenly a "blues" theme, one that had long haunted him, took possession of him, and he began to play it with the air of someone who has at last found what he was looking for. This brief and melancholy theme fitted exactly into the middle section of the rhapsody. The *Rhapsody in Blue* was now virtually completed.

In three weeks he completed the rhapsody, with Ferde Grofe at his elbow, preparing the orchestration while the ink was still wet on the page. Gershwin revised till the last minute; so did Grofe. There were four or five complete rehearsals at the Palais Royal with Gershwin playing the piano, and a number of changes were introduced into the rehearsals, the most important being the insertion of a rising passage ending in a *fermata*, suggested by Victor Herbert. Not all the score was written down. Since the piano solo part was to be played by Gershwin at the concert, and he knew exactly at what point he could improvise, he simply left a gap on the manuscript and told Whiteman "to wait for a nod" where the orchestra was to come in. It was a palpably dangerous arrangement, but it had the virtue of adding freshness to the material.

On the morning of the concert Whiteman suffered from a failure of nerve. He was very frightened. He had spent a large amount of his own money, hired nine additional musicians, and he was beginning to wonder whether there were advantages in abandoning the concert. He had invited the most famous musicians of the time to attend. Rachmaninoff, Godowsky, Stokowski, Walter Damrosch, Jascha Heifetz, Mischa Elman, John Philip

Sousa, John McCormack, and Igor Stravinsky had all been invited, and all had accepted the invitation. By midday he was a little calmer, but in the early afternoon, when snow began falling, he was more worried than ever. He went to the entrance of Aeolian Hall, saw a huge mob of people clamouring to get in, and thought he had come to the wrong place, until he saw Victor Herbert struggling in the crowd. He learned the next day that the house could have been sold ten times over.

He was more depressed than ever when he went back-stage. He vowed he would give $5,000 if he could stop the performance, which had already cost him $7,000. He was not particularly impressed by the programme he was offering, and even had some doubts about the *Rhapsody in Blue*. It was a very strange programme beginning with "Livery Stable Blues" and ending with Sir Edward Elgar's *Pomp and Circumstance*. Of the twenty-six numbers, Gershwin's was the twenty-fifth. Included among the numbers was a semi-symphonic arrangement of Irving Berlin's "Orange Blossoms in California", and a suite of serenades in Spanish, Chinese, and Cuban styles. Twenty-three musicians formed the ensemble. It was a very long programme, and an exceedingly pretentious one.

The most boring part of the programme was the long introductory address by Hugh Ernst which described the educational nature of the programme and the singular validity of Paul Whiteman's orchestra, which was encouraging and bringing to birth a new form of American music. It was not unlike those addresses which are heard periodically in high school auditoriums, and the audience began to be restless. It was more restless than ever by the time the entr'acte came along. The hall was overheated, and the standees were beginning to make their way out. Fatigue, inertia, the most exquisite configurations of boredom had set in when at long last Paul Whiteman, himself bored and confused and close to tears, announced the first public performance of the *Rhapsody in Blue*.

Gershwin stepped out from the wings and took his place at the piano. He shot a single glance at the conductor, and then the baton was raised sharply to introduce the long clarinet wail, like the sound of a steam whistle as a train emerges from a tunnel or like the sound of an explosion in the brain, which introduces the rhapsody. Ross Gorman was Whiteman's clarinettist, and he played those

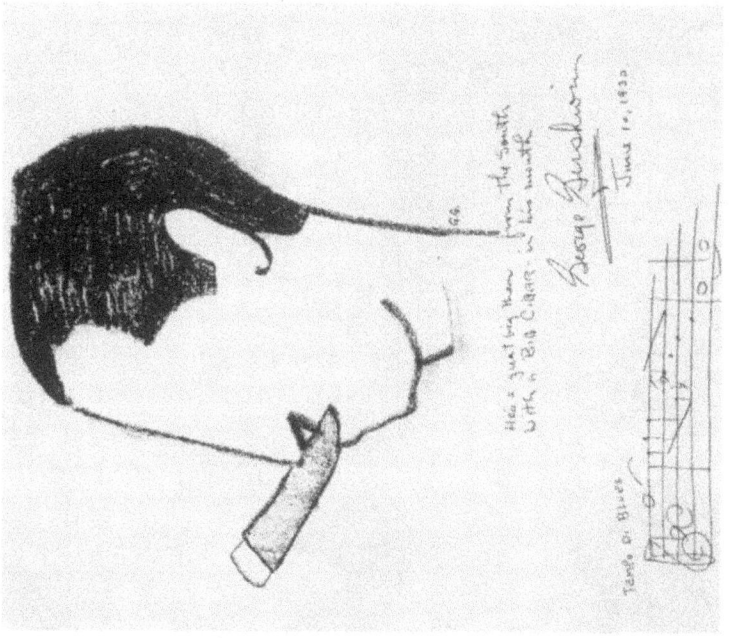

Self-caricature in the possession of Jules Glaenzer

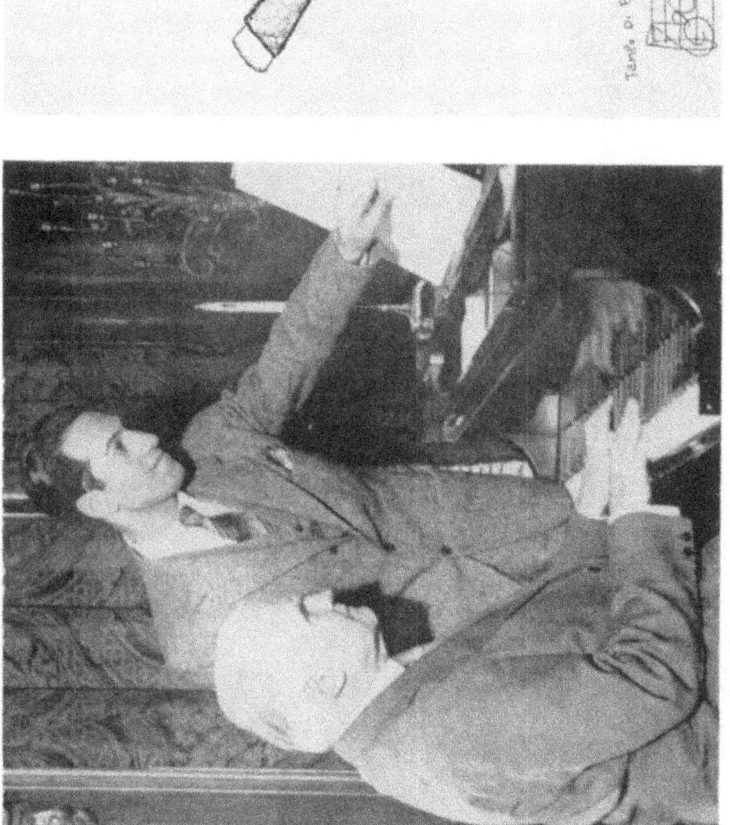

George Gershwin standing by Walter Damrosch at the piano

George Gershwin at Los Angeles, 1937

seventeen broken notes brilliantly, bringing the audience immediately to attention. The audience craned forward. Something new and startling was being performed, all the more desirable because it had come after a long period of waiting. Half-way through Paul Whiteman lost his place and surrendered to a sudden inexplicable fit of weeping. He recovered himself some eleven pages later, and afterward he wondered how the orchestra had performed during the interval. At the end there was an ovation. Gershwin hurried off the stage to bandage his fingers. He had pounded so hard that there was blood on the keys.

The *Rhapsody in Blue* was written in haste and performed without sufficient rehearsals. It was a bravura piece, but it shone with a dazzling light. It was urgent and insistent, but what he was urgently trying to say, and insistently repeating, remained unknown, for so many things were bound up in it that it was impossible to discern a single theme or a single idea embracing the whole. Between the drunken warwhoop at the beginning and the confused battle noises at the end there was a pot-pourri of various styles, all of them recognizably Gershwin's.

Heard freshly, the rhapsody suggests a self-portrait, an attempt by the artist to set down the limits of his entire self-knowledge and his comprehension of the universe. There is the sense of revelation, and of nothing being held back. There is something mystical and trance-like in its statement. What he says is never clear, but that he is attempting to say something important and urgent is evident. It possesses the inevitability which often accompanies works of art constructed in haste.

With some exceptions the critics delighted in it. Olin Downes in the *New York Times* paid it the tribute of a long commentary. He noted how closely it derived from Liszt, and how Gershwin was so often defeated by his own technical immaturity. He noted, too, an alarming *naïveté* and a curious tendency to stress the unimportant passages while passing quickly over passages which deserved to be explored: these were faults that were native to Gershwin and would remain with him to the end. But Downes had no doubt about the importance of the *Rhapsody*. "It is fresh and new," he wrote, "and full of future promise." He found an "Oriental twist to the whole business", meaning perhaps a groundswell of Jewish musical ideas; there was a strange *foreignness* about it, which other musical critics also noted. Deems Taylor in the *World* spoke of its crudity, but he meant the crudity of power and the sacrifice of scoring to momentary effect. He said the *Rhapsody* "had all the faults one might expect from an experimental work—diffuseness, want of self-criticism, and structural uncertainty; but it also revealed a genuine harmonic gift and a piquant and individual harmonic sense to lend significance to its rhythmic ingenuity".

There were, of course, other critics who regarded the *Rhapsody* without affection and with some horror. Its aimlessness offended some, its bravura character offended others. Pitts Sanborn spoke of "the empty passage-work and meaningless repetitions". Lawrence Gilman delighted in the qualities of daring, imagination, and ingenuity, but he was appalled by the triteness of the melodies: "How trite and feeble and conventional the tunes are, how sentimental and vapid the harmonic treatment, under its disguise of fussy and futile counterpoint...."

So they wrote, while the music was still fresh in their ears, before constant repetition made it impossible to hear the music cleanly. We know it too well to be able to disentangle the trite from the unconventional. Like a love affair in our half-forgotten youth it has become a part of our lives, to be remembered with a grave affection and the knowledge that we can never escape from it. And like those love affairs, we tell ourselves that it was drab and wonderfully exciting, and often silly, and troublesome, and heart-warming.

We are so accustomed to hearing it, and are so penetrated with its rhythms, that we forget the awkwardness which nearly all the early commentators saw in it—that awkwardness which is a large part of its charm. It is a thing of promise, depicting a state of mind which belongs wholly to its time, even though it borrows from other times: borrows so much in fact that Isaac Goldberg, the most understanding of commentators, could say, "The pattern of the *Rhapsody*? Liszt. Harmonic devices? Some of them Chopin and Debussy. The blues suggestion? Handy. The slow melody, Tchaikowsky." It was not, of course, as simple as that, for the influences fuse together in remarkably intricate patterns and sometimes we are made aware of influences which are only partially absorbed and others which are rejected. The *Rhapsody* was a firework display, but some of the trains of gunpowder were exploded by accident.

The *Rhapsody* remains a complex work, with many different strands of meaning. It is a train journey, a portrait, a lament for lost youth, a technical extravaganza, an exercise in nostalgia, an experiment in symphonic form, an attempt towards self-criticism. It is infinitely variable, depending on the mood of the listener: never primitive or simple. Self-consciousness enters into all its facets. It came to birth under the oddest circumstances, for it was designed for Paul Whiteman's "Experiment in Modern Music" to demonstrate the validity of jazz, and the *Rhapsody* was not in any real sense jazz at all. Almost inevitably the jazz experts came to regard it as a bastard work.

Four years after the first performance, when the excitement had died down, Constant Lambert wrote an article describing how jazz had disintegrated under the pressures of commercial music:

> Jazz has long ago lost the simple gaiety of the charming savages to whom it owes its birth, and is now, for the most part, a reflection of the nerves, sex-repressions, inferiority complexes and general dreariness of the modern world. The nostalgia of the Negro who wants to go home has given place to the infinitely more weary nostalgia of the cosmopolitan Jew who has no home to go to.

The statement is untrue, but it is not wholly untrue: a strange nostalgia informs nearly all of Gershwin's music. The ghost is always appearing in the middle of those gay parties which come into existence whenever Gershwin sits down at the piano—the ghost only stays for a moment, but clouds of terror hang on the air among the balloons, the confetti and the paper streamers after he has gone. All through the twenties and early thirties the ghosts attended the feast.

With *Rhapsody in Blue* out of the way, Gershwin returned to the more conventional tasks of musical comedy. He wrote *Scandals of 1924* for George White—Vernon Duke ghosted a black-and-white ballet scene for the Tiller girls so well that no one detected any difference—and went on to compose the music for *Primrose* which was performed in London and included the miraculously happy and silly song "Isn't It Terrible What They Did To Mary Queen of Scots?" Before settling down to write serious music, he wrote the scores for four more musical comedies —*Lady Be Good, Tell Me More, Tip Toes* and *The Song of the*

Flame. Most of the songs in these comedies have fallen into oblivion, but there are memorable exceptions. *Lady Be Good* had "Fascinatin' Rhythm" and "So Am I?" *Tell Me More* had "My Fair Lady", a title which was to become more familiar in another context many years later. *Tip Toes* had "That Certain Feeling" and "Looking for a Boy". *The Song of the Flame*, with a book vaguely based on Russian themes, had nothing: the composer seems to have been bored with it even before he began the work. All these musical comedies were successful, and one of them ran for two years in London.

That perhaps was the trouble. The art of musical comedy writing came to him too easily. He usually wrote only the piano score and paid an arranger to orchestrate it. He possessed a recognizable musical comedy style, which could be imitated and "ghosted", and sometimes was. He was always composing songs; there were drawers full of them; and it is in the nature of musical comedy that a song which is not quite suitable in one will find a home in another. So it happened that the most haunting of his love songs, "The Man I Love" was rejected from three musical comedies and became famous only when Lady Mountbatten introduced it in England and started it on its wave of popularity through France and Germany and finally to America.

Gershwin was a happy victim of the song-maker's craft. He enjoyed the independence of his songs, which could be fitted neatly into almost any musical comedy. In his time the story was secondary, and could always be manipulated in accordance with the demands of the music. He could interpolate a song here, and another there, re-arranging them at his leisure. The songs might be fresh, but they were often arranged artificially, with one eye on the music publishers. Song-making was a trade, and there was sometimes a deadly monotony in those songs which were uniformly gay, brisk, nervous and charming.

Yet they were songs that mirrored their time: beneath those shimmering and contrived contours lay a sense of inadequacy, of hesitation, even of menace. Something was always being left unsaid. There was no passion, no opening of the heart. Over the singers lay a sky painted in blue watercolours, and under their feet floated acres of thin ice. Sometimes there could be heard a confused and generalized cry of "Help!" but the voice was so muted that it was easily drowned in the reverberations of the music.

The songs had a purpose—they were intended to be sung in the half-darkness of night-clubs or on the brilliantly-lit stage, and very few of them were whistled in the streets, and none ever achieved the popularity of "Swanee". The great songs came later with *Porgy and Bess*. To hear them sung by Ella Fitzgerald is to hear them in a medium far removed from the age when they were written: she has given them a roundness and an openness lacking in the originals. In the twenties and thirties the appropriate voice was reedy and hoarse with cigarette smoke, plaintive, uncomforting. The jazz age had a curiously tinny sound, with little warmth in it.

That warmth, which is so often lacking in the songs, appears however in the longer compositions. There was warmth, and to spare, in the *Rhapsody in Blue*. In the *New York Concerto*, which he later called the *Concerto in F*, there is so much warmth that we have the curious impression that Gershwin found himself uncomfortable among the flames. It was begun in the summer of 1924 and completed in November. Most of it was composed in a piano practice shack in Chautauqua, where Gershwin spent his mornings alone, surrendering his afternoons to the students who flocked round him in the hope of hearing him improvise.

Nothing he ever wrote suggests so much promise as this scintillating concerto, where for the first time we are made aware of an authentic voice under strict control. The *Rhapsody in Blue* might conceivably have been composed by a brilliant amateur; the concerto is by a professional. The rhapsodic element is absent, or rather it appears only at the end, in its proper place. Here and there we meet the obvious and inevitable flaws—indecision, meaningless bridge-passages, diffused statements. Sometimes he seems to be groping unhappily for themes which escape him until he captures them at last in blind fury; and then when he pins the poor butterflies down on the paper, the colour brushes off from their wings. But those passages are rare. For the most part, and especially in the beautiful second movement, we are made aware of statements made humbly and cleanly. Passion breaks through. There is a quality of humanity, which we will not hear again until he comes to *Porgy and Bess*.

Gershwin had almost no gift for writing, and most of his published statements read a little like schoolboys' themes. His brief analytical description of the *Concerto in F* is among the best of his writings. The flesh is stripped away: everything is cut to the bone. A few days before the opening performance of the concerto, he wrote for the *Tribune*:

> The first movement employs the Charleston rhythm. It is quick and pulsating, representing the young enthusiastic spirit of American life. It begins with a rhythmic motif given out by the kettledrums, supported by other percussion instruments, and with a Charleston motif introduced by bassoon, horns, clarinet and violas. The principal theme is announced by the bassoon. Later, a second theme is introduced by the piano.
>
> The second movement has a poetic nocturnal atmosphere which has come to be referred to as the American blues, but in a purer form than that in which they are usually treated.
>
> The final movement reverts to the style of the first. It is an orgy of rhythms, starting violently and keeping to the same pace throughout.

So, writing in a kind of algebra, Gershwin describes a work which sometimes sings with incomparable brilliance. One listens to the mysterious second movement with surprise, wondering what led him to write so abundantly out of the heart, with no attempt to impose his own appealing patterns, allowing the music to flow freely, as a river flows. It is all poetry, rooted in New York, the light breaking over the city or the dusk falling, the city coming to life or going to sleep, which is only another kind of life. New York is at its most majestic at sunrise and sunset, and Gershwin has caught the shape of the descending and ascending light in music that sings like a hymn or a prayer. True, the prayer will become a Charleston, but so had the prayers of Beethoven in the posthumous quartets become country dance tunes. The style here is Debussy, but Debussy at an infinite remove. Only in the orgiastic third movement are we made aware of an element foreign to the concerto form, for there are passages which read like the brassy overtures which introduce musical comedies, but even these passages have their place—New York has a stridency which can only be expressed by brass.

Again and again one comes back to the wonderful second movement, on which Gershwin expended more care than on any other comparable piece of music, writing slowly and steadily through the summer and fall. There is a shimmering gaiety, a quietness, a sense of worlds unfolding. He is saying what has to be said, and there is the faintest suggestion that he is saying a Jewish prayer; but it may not be a prayer at all. There is ease and control and ripeness, and all these will vanish, for the tricks of the jazz age will return. The brilliant jazzed-up finale seems to have no obvious relation to what has gone before. It is loud and crude, and so it was intended to be, with a roughness unusual even for Gershwin. He had written his second concerto; there was to be one more, and then no others.

The first performance of the *Rhapsody in Blue* took place during a snowstorm; the first performance of the *Concerto in F* took place during a thunderstorm, on the afternoon of December 3, 1925, at Carnegie Hall. The large audience listened patiently through Glazounov's *Fifth Symphony* and Henri Rabaud's *Suite Anglaise*. There was the inevitable thunderous applause when Gershwin, who played the piano solo, took his bows. But the next morning's newspapers greeted the event with appropriate confusion. Only a few critics believed they had heard enduring music. Olin Downes thought it much less original than the *Rhapsody in Blue*, and Lawrence Gilman thought it "trite, at its worst a little dull". Today it has become the commonplace of musical repertory and is likely to endure as long as anything Gershwin ever wrote.

He had showed at last that he could master his craft. It had still to be decided whether he would take the mountains by storm, or whether he would continue to wander pleasantly in the foothills.

5

Portrait of a Composer on a High Trapeze

"ONE CAN FALL into the heights as well as into the depths," said the great German poet Friedrich Hölderlin, and there is a sense in which Gershwin fell with a roar into the utmost heights possible to a man in his generation. He would hardly have been human if he had not been shaken by the experience. He was the most celebrated composer of his time, the wealthiest, the most prodigal with his talents. No one quite like him had ever appeared on the American scene, and no one like him ever came again. He was one of those rare men who gather strength from the limelight and are not blinded by it.

There were flaws in the surface, of course: so many of them that he sometimes gives the appearance of a man about to crumble into a pinch of dust. Sometimes the crisp tone falters, and we are made aware of the presence of a much older voice weighed down with unalterable melancholy, the voice of an ancient rabbi in some remote province of Poland; but this voice appeared only in his music, and no one ever heard it from his lips. Outwardly he was the gayest of mortals, charged with electricity, happy only when he was surrounded by friends. He hated loneliness, and feared it. He never saw himself as a spectator; he saw himself as a spectacle. His pride was to challenge all musicians of the past, and he quite seriously regarded himself as "the great innovator". He liked to make pronunciamentos about composers, and he was always reckless in his judgements. He was so absorbed in self-worship that there were times when he must have come perilously close to madness.

In fact he remained astonishingly sane even when he was most triumphantly successful. His family helped; so did his friends; and he was lucky in both. Their protective warmth gave him strength. He was especially close to his father, who could never quite take his fame seriously. One day Gershwin showed him a cheque he had received, for an astronomical sum in dollars. "Do you really think you are worth it, George?" his father asked, and broke out in hesitant, nervous laughter. Shown the manuscript of the *Rhapsody in Blue* and told that it represented another astronomical sum, he said, "I suppose it must be good—it takes twenty minutes to play, doesn't it?" In his quiet way he liked cutting things down to size; and many of the stories humorously told against him—his whimsical comments on the behaviour of the fashionable "young things" who flocked to his son's studio—could as well be told in his favour. He possessed a prodigious gaiety. He would spend hours fashioning and refashioning a joke, and he liked telling "pratfall" jokes in which he was the amused spectator of his own downfall. When his son took an expensive penthouse apartment on Riverside Drive, it amused him to put on the uniform of the elevator man and watch the arrival of distinguished guests from the anonymity of his uniform. For him life was a theatre, and he enjoyed the passing scene without ever identifying himself with it. Life was like one of those dramas performed by Boris Thomashefsky, and he was hugely delighted by everything he saw.

If Morris Gershwin was quicksilver, Rose Gershwin was iron. She had drive and energy, and was consumed with restless ambitions which were never satisfied. She gave the appearance of someone who has never quite accustomed herself to the world. She was always on the move. Alert, knowledgeable, pretentious, puzzled by her son's occasional addiction to music which was not immediately profitable, she followed the pattern of the matriarch who sees her sons outgrow her influence. She could be as hard as nails about money, but she was a warm hostess, presiding over the dining-table with exquisite manners. It was one of her major griefs that George, who suffered from "a composer's stomach", could rarely eat the meals she put before him.

Ira was the balance wheel, calm, reflective, rarely giving way to emotions. He would have made a good professor if he had not, out of laziness, given up the courses he took at Columbia. He knew more about the dregs of life than his brother would ever know, for he had taken odd jobs in bathhouses and restaurants, hating every moment of it. He loved books to distraction. He was the eternal student, who failed at his studies, and went on to fail at a succession of improbable jobs. For a while he was the cashier of a travelling carnival owned by Kokomo Jimmy; he was a darkroom worker, an attendant at Altman's, a reviewer of vaudeville. He wrote lyrics when he worked in a bathhouse, and went on writing lyrics and short poetical pieces for magazines even though he had little hope of seeing them published. About the time of *La La Lucille* he began to see that there was a place for a lyricist in commercial music, and he trained himself to become an accomplished lyricist long before he was permitted to write the lyrics for *Lady Be Good*, where for the first time he appeared on the programme under his own name. Between Ira and George there was an extraordinary empathy: they thought the same thoughts and looked at the world in the same way, though they saw it from different heights. George was closest to his father; after his father came Ira.

The protective net around George was already formed by the time *Rhapsody in Blue* came to be written. He already knew the friends he would rely on—Carl Van Vechten, Jules Glaenzer, Lou Paley, Bill Daly, Henry Botkin, who was his cousin, and the rest of the small intimate circle which revolved around him as a catherine wheel revolves around its fiery centre. A little later came Kay Swift, young and ebullient, wonderfully quick-witted as her mind bounced happily from one surprised idea to another. She seemed to have solved the problem of perpetual motion. Small and delicate, with an unruffled beauty, she was one of the few with whom he enjoyed playing classical duets: they would play Bach fugues together, and go on to play Beethoven variations until it seemed that they would never end. She was also one of the few people around him who possessed a basic training in music.

Vernon Duke was another. Young and almost terrifyingly elegant, he was the only man who ever made the journey from Constantinople to New York by way of "Swanee". He was intoxicated with classical Russian music. He arrived in America with dreams of writing endless symphonies and songs based on the poems of Pushkin, and soon found himself close to starvation. Gershwin admired him and took him along to Max Dreyfus, the high priest of musical comedy, with a suite of offices out of which commercial music rolled like an illimitable flood, but when Vernon Duke played a song which Gershwin admired there was no offer of employment. Still, Gershwin was helpful, and Vernon Duke found himself gainfully employed as a "ghost" and as an arranger of Gershwin songs. "Try to write some real popular tunes," Gershwin told him. "They will open you up!"

In the eyes of Vernon Duke, Gershwin was the supreme example of the composer who had "opened up". He had found the secret of creation. It was a very simple secret—the pure *improvisatore* sitting down at the piano and improving would follow his ideas until they reached their inevitable conclusion, and the task of the composer was simply to recognize amid the host of ideas displayed by the music the one idea which possessed a sustaining power. For hours Vernon Duke watched the process of creation taking place. Gershwin never changed tempo, never played rubato; he simply forged forward at a relentless 4/4 beat, until with so much accumulated power behind him it became almost physically impossible for him to stop. He would close his eyes and intone one of Ira's lyrics, "pushing out his lips in an oddly Negroid manner." There was about all his singing a curious incantatory quality.

Gershwin's strange singing, his odd nervous laughter, his perpetual concern with his stomach, for he fed largely on bran and the most easily digestible foods, suggest a man with a load of neurotic mischief. In fact, he showed few signs of neurosis. He was well-built and singularly poised, and almost never gave way to exhibitions of temper. There was a natural nobility in his bearing. Dorothy Heyward thought he looked like "a young Jewish prince". When he came to live on Riverside Drive there was usually a crowd of admirers and job-seekers waiting in an ante-room for a glimpse of him; and when he came out of the studio, he showed a happy knack of putting everyone at ease. He had a word for everyone. He was perfectly conscious of his fame, and there was always the suggestion of a small but calculable distance between the famous composer and the admirer, but there was no sense of *hauteur*. Fame, which hurts many, helped him to grow. He seems to have enjoyed his fame all the more because he seems to have known he would enjoy it only for a short while.

His manners were distinguished. There was, when he was in fashionable company, a courtliness about him, a sense of decorum and propriety which he sometimes carried to excess. It was Jules Glaenzer who first pointed out to him the inadvisability of talking to a woman with a cigar in his mouth. From Jules Glaenzer he learned the proper clothes to wear in high society, and how to address duchesses, and how to eat off gold plate. That courtly *bon vivant*, who had been everywhere and knew everyone, introduced him to the Duke of Kent and the Mountbattens, and saw to it that he saw everyone worth seeing in Paris and New York. In his fashionable apartment in Paris Glaenzer assembled *le haut monde* whenever Gershwin came to town; and when Glaenzer came to live in New York as the manager of Cartier's, the diamond merchants, there were more parties in his exquisite apartment on 65th Street and Lexington Avenue. The champagne flowed; Gertrude Lawrence sang; Moss Hart beamed; the two grand pianos at the far end of the concert room were constantly being pounded. Gershwin regarded it as one of the minor ironies of fate that he was not provided with four hands, so that he could play both the grand pianos at once.

Jules Glaenzer had the habit of effacing himself. He liked to watch from the shadows, as from the wings, the progress of his parties. "Gershwin was my best pupil," he said recently. "He was wonderful—never made a mistake and charmed everyone. But no one could ever get him away from the piano." Only once did Glaenzer see Gershwin under adverse circumstances. That was in an aeroplane between London and Paris, when Gershwin was green with misery, and threatening never to go up in an aeroplane again. "He was all right when he came down, but he was sick to the gills during the flight, and he was praying hard. He wouldn't look out. Just sat there with his face pinched with horror. Hated me, hated everything. I don't think I've ever seen a man looking so downcast in his life. We cheered him up with some good food, and then showed him the town, Maxim's, bordellos, everything."

Jules Glaenzer kept a guest book which recorded the signatures of his guests and sometimes their comments. The famous names sweep across the page. There is Noel Coward's signature, so intricate a thing that it looks like a complex mechanical design. There is Gertrude Lawrence dancing magnificently across a whole page. Gershwin's signatures are small at the beginning, but grew impressively larger as he became more famous. Usually they are accompanied by a cramped pen drawing of his own profile—a sad little drawing, all nose and cigar, as large as a postage stamp. But when he gave himself space, as in the drawing illustrated in this book, he could draw himself brilliantly in three seconds. He was still all nose and cigar, but the sadness had gone. He needed elbow room.

After the *Rhapsody in Blue* he was almost the most famous person in New York, lionized by all the wealthy hostesses. He did not wait to be asked to play when invited to parties. He was never bothered if other musicians were present. He would assume that he alone deserved to sit at the piano. In Gershwin's view this was not selfishness. He felt it would be an intolerable outrage if others played.

The lion did not roar: the lion simply played the piano until his music became part of the air men breathed, as familiar as wine. There were non-stop performances lasting from seven o'clock in the evening to the early hours of the morning. Gently, relentlessly, tirelessly, he insisted on playing his music, and no one ever denied him this pleasure for the excellent reason that he filled the music with his own overflowing vitality. "People were reborn when he played," Kay Swift remembers. "It was like getting a double shot of B12."

He glowed especially at the parties given by his friend Carl Van Vechten. Emily Clark has described a June evening at one of those parties in the large apartment on 54th Street:

> There was George Gershwin playing and singing bits from his current musical show to a crowd of people, among whom Theodore Dreiser sat, heavy and brooding, the direct antithesis, almost a contradiction of all that Gershwin means. And Elinor Wylie sat, aloof and lively, a contradiction and denial of all that both Dreiser and Gershwin mean. Later some woman danced, and later still Paul Robeson sang. Last of all, James Weldon Johnson recited his "Go Down, Death". And Carl hovered about in doorways, as always on such evenings, benevolent and shining.

Gershwin too was benevolent and shining as he strode into the limelight. He usually stayed there. Carl Van Vechten remembers a period when Gershwin came nearly every night to his apartment, calling beforehand to ask permission to bring a girl friend —nearly always a different one—and then playing the piano half the night as though he had no other ambition in life than to entertain, always performing variations on the themes of the songs in the musical comedies, always bursting with vitality. "There was a wonderful fire in him," Carl Van Vechten recalled recently. "The room would light up when he came in. There was an astonishing vitality in him. You were intimate with him the moment you saw him, and he had thousands of intimate friends."

That was one side of the picture, but there were many others. Sometimes the engaging boyish quality vanished, and there was the deeply puzzled hypochondriac who complained bitterly about his health, but these moments rarely lasted for long. More disturbing were the flashes of pride, the ferocious commands, the exhibitions of ill-temper, which must have had their origins in some defensive mechanism. Once in New York in the presence of Carl Van Vechten he was telling Serge Koussevitsky about a performance of one of his own works in Brooklyn. "You'll simply have to attend," Gershwin said. "It would be intolerable if you didn't. You've got to go this afternoon." It was a naked command, unaccompanied by any suggestion that tickets or transport would be made available to the conductor, who had other things to do than to make a special journey to Brooklyn.

Countless similar stories were told about his free-wheeling pride. Oscar Levant was once travelling with him in a train to Pittsburgh. They were talking amiably about music, and Levant was looking forward to a long evening of discussion. Suddenly Gershwin began to undress and slipped into a lower berth. "Lower berth, upper berth," said Gershwin. "That's the difference between talent and genius."

Some time later, at one of those parties where Gershwin played the piano watched by an audience "absorbed with the fascinated attentiveness of a Stormtrooper listening to one of Hitler's well-modulated firehouse chats", Oscar Levant had his revenge. He said quietly, "Tell me, George, if you had to do it all over again, would you fall in love with yourself again?" On another occasion Oscar Levant heard Gershwin describing a charming girl: "She has a little love for everyone and not a great deal for anybody." Levant had the sinking feeling that Gershwin was unconsciously describing himself.

He demanded worship, and was worshipped wherever he went. Women clustered round him, and he demanded from them the same absolute worship he received when he was playing the piano. Inevitably the women rebelled. They, too, wanted worship; they floated away and were replaced by others; a succession of mistresses danced fleetingly through his life.

He knew that something was wrong, and turned to psychiatrists for help. They were unable to help him, or fell under his spell. The parade of mistresses continued, underscoring his essential restlessness.

According to one of the psychiatrists who treated him, Gershwin's attitude to sex was comparable with that of a healthy and irresponsible adolescent. He enjoyed sexual encounters for their own sake and because they stimulated him to compose new musical themes. He was not unkind to his mistresses; it was simply that he felt he had a right to use them as part of his exploration of musical experience. He was a sexual athlete and sometimes slept with two women at once in his bed.

An adolescent quality remained with him to the end. He had the bounce, the charm, the vitality of an adolescent. He was a supreme egotist and the delighted spectator of his own fame. He knew better than anyone his exact position in the hierarchy of musicians in his time, and since he was at the very top and was assured of survival, he felt no qualms about claiming his rights. He was like the lord of the manor whose claim to the *jus primu noctu* is based on his patent of nobility.

In all this Gershwin was the child of his time. His morals were no better or worse than those of the society he lived in. Coming to maturity in "the splendid Drunken Twenties"—the phrase is Carl Van Vechten's—he was himself splendidly drunk with the effervescence of the age. It was the time of jazz, speakeasies, trial marriages and casual love affairs, of *Tender Is the Night* and *The Great Gatsby*, of Harriet Monroe and Mencken and the young Lindbergh. It was very good to be alive in those days, but no one seems to have known what he was living for. In that aimless paradise there were no angels with flaming swords.

The angels with flaming swords came later; meanwhile there was the delirious dance to the light of candles burning at both ends and the sense that it would all come to an end much sooner than anyone expected. "It was all gay, irresponsible and meaningless, perhaps, but *gay*," said Carl Van Vechten's Peter Whiffle. But sometimes gaiety could be overwhelmingly sorrowful, and sometimes the dancers found themselves still dancing in the early morning with the cold light of dawn coming through the windows of the bedraggled ballroom.

While Gershwin's music reflected the gaiety of the age, it also reflected its emptiness, its incoherence, its essential pessimism. There was about it, very often, the sweet smell of corruption and death. The tripping notes would be followed by a "blues" passage, and then the tripping notes would be resumed, to give place to a sudden scream from the clarinets and a kind of hovering over the original "blues" passage. The effect of the music was to exasperate the senses, quickening them until they flagged from sheer exhaustion, but at the moment when exhaustion was reached there would be another lively and clean-cut adagio passage to cut through the gloom. Taken in large quantities, Gershwin's music acted on the senses like alcohol and heroin. It became a drug, and everyone became an addict.

Gershwin himself was a little puzzled by his success. He would ask people what it was that distinguished his music from others' and why he had been skyrocketed to fame, when his musical resources were so rudimentary. He hankered after respectability, studied the scores of the masters, and consulted established musicians to find out whether anything was wrong. He told Serge Koussevitsky, "I've only one object—to be a great musician, and I mean great!" Beneath the mask of gaiety was a man consumed with ambition to write music that would last beyond his own time.

That driving ambition fed on his sense of inadequacy, and tortured him. He was perfectly aware of the dangers inherent in his facility. He knew to a hairbreadth exactly how far he could go without the aid of a much greater fund of musical knowledge than he possessed. He was deadly serious in his determination to acquire knowledge. One day he met the distinguished composer Edgar Varèse, and asked to become his student. "I can't help you," Varèse said kindly. "We're going in different directions. We have nothing in common musically." Varèse admired his talents, but seems to have felt that nothing would be gained by a music which had its roots in the orchestra pit of the musical comedy stage.

Gershwin was luckier with the young composer Henry Cowell, who combined a natural warmth with extraordinary precision. In San Francisco, Cowell had known the family of Ira's wife, Leonore Strunsky, and felt a paternal interest in the Gershwin family. He had no illusions about Gershwin's lack of musical knowledge. Over a period of two years he went once or twice a week to Gershwin's apartment, giving him exercises to do.

There would be the inevitable arguments about historic counterpoint, and Cowell would point out the established tradition, while Gershwin would argue against all traditions.

To Cowell's astonishment Gershwin seemed unable to hear written music in his head, and had no fundamental talent for recognizing notes as tones. "He had a fantastic ear," Cowell said recently. "When I first met him, he had almost no knowledge of the theory of counterpoint or harmony. He knew harmony by ear, and most of the time he was right, but he could be terribly wrong. He used to say, 'I'm crazy with ideas, and don't know what to do next.' He was always in a terrible hurry, and he always regarded himself as a master. He absolutely believed he could combine classical music with popular music. Once when we were arguing about the history of music, he said, 'What's it all about? I'm history.' He was like that. There was tension in his music and in his voice; he was always scurrying to get the words out, always hurrying to finish one thing and get on with the next. He had tremendous gifts, but did not always know what to do with them."

Cowell was one of the very few who could see Gershwin in perspective. It amused him a little to hear Gershwin saying one moment, "I am history," and then adding in the next breath, "I am a man without traditions." The two statements were not incompatible. Gershwin would throw history away, only to discover that it was always coming back again. He waged a continual war against history, and it seems rarely to have occurred to him that he was part of the historical process.

On different occasions Gershwin would attempt to describe his place in music, and the place of his fellow-composers. Usually his statements were characterized by a quite extraordinary awkwardness. Sometimes his theories led him to irresponsible conclusions, as when he spoke of the relationship between music and the emotions:

> People in the underworld, dope fiends and gun men invariably are music lovers, and if not, they are affected by it. Music is entering into medicine. Music sets up a certain vibration which unquestionably results in a physical reaction. Eventually the proper vibration for everyone will be found and utilized. I like to think of music as an emotional science.

He could be equally childish when he made *ex cathedra* statements about the dangerous corruptive influences of radio and the phonograph. In his view the radio and the phonograph were harmful because they gave currency to much cheap music, but the good composer would never be corrupted by them; in some mysterious fashion the good composer lived above the temptations of the crowd. Schubert, had he lived into the present age, would have been well-rewarded:

> Schubert did not make any money because he did not have an opportunity through the means of distribution of his day to reach the public. He died at the age of thirty-one, and had a certain reputation. If he had lived to be fifty or sixty, unquestionably he would have obtained recognition in his own day. If he were living today, he would be well-off and comfortable.

It is a little too easy, a little too audacious. The spectacle of Schubert writing for the musical comedy stage or playing his music on the radio while an announcer celebrates the virtues of stomach pills is almost beyond our comprehension.

Occasionally, however, Gershwin could be induced to say wise things simply, as when he wrote for Henry Cowell a brief account of the influence of folk music on contemporary musical traditions:

> The great music of the past in other countries has always been built on folk music. This is the strongest source of musical fecundity. America is no exception among the countries. The best music being written today is music which comes from folk sources.
>
> It is not always recognized that America has folk music; yet it really has not only one, but many different folk musics. It is a vast land and different sorts of folk music have sprung up in different parts, all having validity, and all being a possible foundation for development into an art-music. For this reason I believe it is possible for a number of distinctive styles to develop in America, all legitimately born of folk song from different localities. Jazz, ragtime, Negro spirituals and blues, Southern mountain songs, country fiddling and cowboy songs

can all be employed in the creation of American art-music, and are actually used by many composers now . . .

Jazz I regard as an American folk music; not the only one, but a very powerful one which is probably in the blood and feeling of the American people more than any other style of folk music. I believe that it can be made the basis for serious symphonic works of lasting value in the hands of a composer with talent for both jazz and symphonic music.*

Gershwin could perhaps have expressed himself more happily, but the very hesitations and repetitions add to the effect of honesty and candour. There was nothing in the least startling in what he said, but we are startled by his manner of saying it—heavily, as though against the grain, searching even while he is expressing it for some flaw in the argument. There was no flaw; and he knew himself to be the "composer with talent for both jazz and symphonic music".

There was no single thread in Gershwin's life. He was always, as his biographer Isaac Goldberg said, "the young Colossus bestriding American music, with one foot in Tin Pan Alley, and the other in Carnegie Hall." He was split down the middle, and obscurely aware that Tin Pan Alley could be forced into Carnegie Hall only by an act of violence. His attempts to write serious music were rare and occurred at long intervals.

After the *Concerto in F* came *Oh Kay*, starring Gertrude Lawrence and Victor Moore. There was the usual silly story of bootleggers and secret hideouts, with the ageing Victor Moore interminably pursued by blondes; but the score was good with more than the usual number of good songs. There was "Clap Yo' Hands", "Someone To Watch Over Me", and the naughty "Do, Do, Do". "Out of my entire annual output of songs," Gershwin once said, "perhaps two—or at most, three—came as a result of inspiration." Those three were as charming as any he had done, and might reasonably be ascribed to inspiration. *Oh Kay* was followed by *Funny Face*. The hit song was "'S Wonderful", and this too can be ascribed to inspiration. *Oh Kay* ran for 256 performances, and *Funny Face* had an almost equally long run.

* Henry Cowell, *American Composers on American Music*, p. 186-7, Stanford University Press, 1933.

With the world at his feet Gershwin was enjoying himself. He especially enjoyed his visits to London, where he became the darling of Mayfair and the rival of Noel Coward. He took an apartment in Pall Mall, bought his suits in Savile Row and his hats at Scott's. Gordon Craig tells the story of how it delighted him to have Isadora Duncan sharpening his pencils for him. Gershwin amused himself by visiting his tailors in the company of Gertrude Lawrence, who chose his suits for him and picked out his ties. The Mountbattens and the young Duke of Kent became intimate friends. Vernon Duke, then in London, watched the passage of the meteor with a sense of mounting wonder. Almost Gershwin was the toast of England. He was showered with invitations to parties. Every night he played the piano to an attentive audience. "George's superb piano playing took London completely by storm," Vernon Duke said. "Clubmen, guardees, and debutantes surrounded the American Liszt, architect of musical skyscrapers and the first transatlantic composer with a voice of his own." Gershwin especially enjoyed the crowning honour—a signed photograph of the Duke of Kent with the inscription "From George to George".

All the outward signs of success were at his command. He had wealth, beautiful women, and fast cars; his movements were reported in the society columns; and Elsa Maxwell was fond of him. Wherever he travelled, he was greeted by reporters and society hostesses. Millionaires clamoured to present him with their daughters. He was the owner of an astonishing modernistic penthouse on Riverside Drive. His annual income went well into six figures. Pandora had presented him with everything he could wish for, but he seems to have felt the need of further worlds to conquer. About this time he took up painting.

There was nothing amateurish in his interest in painting. Under the guidance of his cousin Henry Botkin he threw himself into painting with all the pent-up enthusiasm of a convert. He possessed extraordinary powers of concentration. He could paint under any conditions, anywhere, jumping from the piano to the easel and back again. He was not satisfied with being an ordinary painter. "If he saw you juggling two coffee pots he would start practising to be a juggler," Kay Swift recalls. "By evening he would be the best coffee-pot juggler in the world." So it was with his painting.

His painting was like his music, exuberant, impulsive, compelling. He was an excellent portraitist, though he tended to show his sitters in moods of unrestrained melancholy, and he rarely portrayed more than the head and the shoulders, as though he could not be bothered with the rest of the human animal. He painted clothes lumpily, which was odd, because he dressed well and took a serious interest in clothes. He painted neckties like swollen sausages, and was often lazy with backgrounds. But there is no doubt that he was well on his way to becoming a serious painter.

His most famous painting, which was also his most successful, was a self-portrait. He stands before the easel, wearing a shining top hat, an immaculate starched shirt, and full evening dress, as though he had just entered the studio to put a few finishing touches to the picture while on his way to a concert. He stands there very gracefully, and there is something about his posture which suggests that he is not anchored firmly to the ground, but poised for flight. At first glance the picture is all innocence, an impression reinforced by the candid gaze he offers to the world. The second glance is more disturbing, for we observe that he is painting himself as he sees himself in the mirror and he has deliberately painted the painting hand and part of the easel in the foreground. There is a suggestion of endlessly reflecting mirrors, of himself receding into the far distance as the last mirror image vanishes, and at the same time, so boldly has he portrayed himself, we are made aware of a man dazzled by his own reflected magnificence. It is the most naked of all his paintings.

Gershwin's bewildering portrait of himself lacks humility, but there was real humility in his portrait of DuBose Heyward, the author of the novel *Porgy*, from which *Porgy and Bess* is derived. DuBose Heyward was a southern aristocrat who suffered an attack of polio; and the crippled Porgy of the novel was in some measure a projection of himself, suffering many of the same agonies and torments from which DuBose Heyward himself suffered. Gershwin's portrait catches the quite extraordinary sensitivity of the aristocratic face. There is fear of pain, and hunger for pain, and a grave quietness. DuBose Heyward's face is alive. In the more famous "Self-portrait" we keep looking for the strings which hold up the dazzling marionette.

Gershwin spent every free moment painting. He told his friend

Patric Farrell, "I paint by ear. I compose my paintings as I compose music." He had a tremendous passion for Rouault's paintings and bought as many as he could afford, saying he wished he could write music as Rouault painted. To the end of his life he would speak of Rouault with bated breath, as of someone possessed by gifts not given to ordinary mortals.

As he collected paintings, so he collected painters. He was always inviting them to stay in his apartment. He was especially friendly with the Mexican artist, David Siqueiros, who stayed with him at Riverside Drive. He commissioned Siqueiros to do a portrait of him. "I want you to do my head," he said, but the head was no sooner begun when Gershwin changed his mind and said he wanted a life-size painting. Siqueiros bought a larger canvas and set to work on the life-size portrait. Gershwin asked whether there was enough room for a piano. "We'll need a larger canvas, if I am going to paint the piano," Siqueiros suggested. The artist bought a new canvas, and had hardly begun when it occurred to Gershwin that it was absurd to have him playing the piano without an audience—why not show him playing at the Metropolitan Opera House? Another and much vaster canvas was bought. Siqueiros painted Gershwin sitting at the piano on the empty stage, playing the *Rhapsody in Blue*, while behind him, streaming into the distance, in tier upon tier, sat the audience in crowded pinpoints of light. The painting has a curious resemblance to Titian's "Last Judgement" in Venice, showing Christ enthroned and surrounded by the souls of the blessed.

When Gershwin saw the finished painting, he was still not satisfied with it. In the front row were his relatives and intimate friends. His father and mother were there. So were Ira and Leonore, and Gershwin's psychiatrist, Dr. Gregory Zilboorg, and Oscar Levant and Henry Botkin, but someone was missing. At last Gershwin decided that the missing person was Siqueiros, who finally painted himself into the picture at the extreme left-hand corner. Gershwin had changed the picture five times until he was satisfied. From a small and intimate portrait the painting had swollen out until it embraced an entire universe.

It was the best painting ever made of Gershwin, and the most mysterious one, for the style and grouping were altogether outside the usual style of Siqueiros. It was much more in the style of Gershwin himself. In a sense he had painted it, using the hand and brush of Siqueiros. For its revelation of character this painting stands as an astonishing companion-piece to the "Self Portrait" completed in the same year.

Gershwin's knowledge of painting was wide-ranging, but restricted to the painters of his own time. He liked paintings that were muscular, flaming with colour, and he especially admired Rouault's clowns, seeing perhaps in those gaunt and ravaged features a mysterious knowledge that was denied to him. He spent hours poring over his collection of paintings, which included Picasso's *The Absinthe Drinker*. There were paintings by Chagall, Modigliani, Gauguin, Rousseau, Dérain, Léger and Kandinsky. Of Americans he enjoyed the lithographs of George Bellows and the paintings of Thomas Hart Benton. Altogether he owned nearly seventy paintings, many of them museum pieces. After his death many of them were bought by museums, *The Absinthe Drinker* going to the Museum of Modern Art in New York.

For Gershwin painting was not a luxury but a necessity. He spent large sums of money on acquiring his collection, and was always prepared to spend more. Friends leaving for Europe were warned to look out for paintings to add to the collection. He would send telegrams: "Get me a Kokoschka," or "Look out for a Picasso for me." He nearly always got what he wanted.

Rarely does it happen that a mind trained in musical ideas can express itself on canvas. Gershwin was the happy exception. Paintings aroused musical ideas in him; and for him music was full of colour. Once when he was shown a Picasso side by side with a Klee, he said, "I can see it now. Picasso is the full orchestra, and Klee is the string quartet."

For him painting was many things—exhilaration, rest from music, a source of energy and knowledge, something which made less demands on his hands than the constant pounding on the piano keys. It was also perhaps a shelter from the coming storms.

6

An American in Paris

NINETEEN-TWENTY-EIGHT was the year before the storm. Calvin Coolidge was President, and America was basking in the sunshine of economic prosperity. Jazz was still the rage. It was the year of Ravel's *Bolero*, and the *Graf Zeppelin* crossing the Atlantic, the Russians beginning their Five Year Plan, and Hitler still unheard-of. Thornton Wilder published *The Bridge of San Luis Rey*, and Arnold Zweig's *The Case of Sergeant Grischa* became a best-seller. Consciences were at rest in the best of all possible worlds.

That year Gershwin made his fifth visit to Europe. In the past he had spent most of his time in London working on his theatrical productions, but this time he came on holiday. He had some vague plans of writing music on European themes and soaking up atmosphere and perhaps studying briefly with Ravel, who had already shown him great cordiality, but there was nothing definite. He would go where the spirit took him, attending a few performances of his own work. It was to be his last visit to Europe. He may have guessed that it would be a triumph.

He spent a little more than a week in London, meeting old friends and attending a George Gershwin evening at the Kit Kat night-club, then the most sought after night-club in the whole of London. He saw the closing performance of *Oh, Kay* with Gertrude Lawrence which had run for a respectable two hundred and fourteen performances. He renewed his friendship with the Duke of Kent and the Mountbattens, went to parties and gave them, and lived in a flat in Pall Mall. He became more English than the English, and even developed a notable English accent. He spent many hours at his Savile Row tailors, and when they had finished with him he could hardly be distinguished from a Guards officer in mufti. He wore a bowler hat and carried an umbrella, and strode along with exactly the right air of extravagant good taste.

But England was a known land, and he was in a hurry to reach

France. With his party, which included his brother Ira and his sister Frances, he took the cross-Channel steamer for France on March 25th. Immediately the pace quickened. There were gala performances, *soirées*, concerts, ballets, meetings with nearly all the great musicians then living in Paris. He met Ravel, Stravinsky, Francis Poulenc, Georges Auric, and Serge Prokofiev. On the last day of March he attended a performance of the *Rhapsody in Blue* conducted by Rhené Baton at the Théâtre Mogador. It was not the best of performances, for the musicians had rehearsed the piece for only half an hour and someone plucked a banjo chord throughout the entire performance and sometimes the fast tempo dragged down to a walking pace. Gershwin was violently uncomfortable and vanished into the bar, only to be called back to receive an ovation. It was the first of many ovations. There was another performance of the *Rhapsody* at the fashionable Théâtre des Champs-Elysées, where it was given in the form of a ballet designed and choreographed by Anton Dolin, an Englishman who danced with a peculiarly Russian verve and brilliance.

At the end of May there was a still greater triumph when the *Concerto in F* was played at the Paris Opera, with Dmitri Tiomkin as soloist. The concerto was given the place of honour, at the end of the programme. All Paris was there; Gershwin was greeted with the inevitable ovation; and there was some shaking of heads. Diaghilev muttered that it was "good jazz but bad Liszt". Prokofiev, a more competent judge, dismissed it with the remark that it consisted of "thirty-two bar choruses rather badly bridged together". However, he had no illusions about Gershwin's gifts as a pianist and composer, and asked Vernon Duke to arrange a meeting. Accordingly Gershwin went to Prokofiev's apartment and played his own music for hours. The old master was impressed, and suggested there was a great future for Gershwin if he would leave "dollars and dinners" alone.

To this period belong two stories which may be apocryphal. According to the first story Gershwin asked Ravel to accept him as a student. Ravel is said to have replied, "What is the point of becoming a second-rate Ravel when you are already a first-rate Gershwin?" According to the second story Gershwin called on Stravinsky at his apartment and asked the same question. There was a short pause, while Stravinsky glanced quizzically at his visitor and then said, "How much do you earn?" Gershwin answered, "Between two and three hundred thousand dollars a year." "Then, my dear friend," Stravinsky replied, "let me take lessons from you."

The stories are almost certainly untrue, but they suggest the formidable stature Gershwin had reached in the eyes of two great European composers. He was basking in glory. In the intervals of rushing about Paris, he was sketching the preliminary drafts of a new orchestral composition commissioned by Walter Damrosch called *An American in Paris*. There is a pleasant legend that he wrote the composition in a few days in Paris, but in fact it had a long gestation. Parts of it were written during a previous visit to Europe, and he had worked on it in New York. Most of the concluding "blues" section was written in Paris, and he was sufficiently advanced with the composition to permit the *New York Times* to announce early in June that *An American in Paris* would be played at Carnegie Hall by the New York Philharmonic Orchestra during the coming season.

Then, to escape the pressing attentions of his admirers, he went off on a visit to Germany and Austria. One night in Germany he attended with George Middleton a performance of the classic Yiddish drama *The Dybbuk*. It made a deep impression on him. He thought very seriously of turning it into an opera, and he would have done so if the rights had been available. The play haunted him. The subject was familiar to him, for similar plays were performed by Boris Thomashefsky in his Second Avenue Theatre. There are passages in *Porgy and Bess* which seem to reflect at a distance the same hauntings which occur in *The Dybbuk*.

The Dybbuk is a play devoted to the strange lunar world which lies between earth and heaven, where unknown powers seek for fulfilment. In the original version it bore the sub-title *Between Two Worlds*. Written by S. An-ski (Shloyme Zalmon Rappoport), it described the evil spirit which had taken root in the soul of Leah and how all the attempts to exorcise the evil spirit end in failure. The evil spirit is, in fact, the soul of a dead man who refuses to leave her even when the shrouds, the horns and the black candles are brought to her and the anathemas are uttered against her. To the Rabbi Azrael, Leah utters her great cry of doom:

> I know that angels and archangels obey your word, but me

you cannot command. I have nowhere to go. Every road is barred against me, and every gate is locked. There is heaven and earth, and all the countless worlds of space, and yet in not one of them is there any place for me.

The greatness of *The Dybbuk* lies in the fact that it deals with elemental things. Gershwin was not yet ready for elemental things, though he would speak about them later in the music of *Porgy and Bess*.

In Austria he continued to work on *An American in Paris*, which sometimes betrays a faint flavour of Viennese chocolate, saturated with whipped cream and sugar. He sat for hours in Madame Sacher's famous coffee house, and wherever he went the musicians seemed to know of his coming and struck up *Rhapsody in Blue*. The highlight of the visit was a tea party given in his honour by the widow of Johann Strauss. As Gershwin liked to tell the story, he made a precipitate retreat when Frau Strauss offered him the manuscript of *Die Fledermaus* for a fantastic sum in dollars.

When he returned to New York in late June, he brought with him eight volumes of Debussy's works and the uncompleted piano score of *An American in Paris*. If he had hoped to get down to work at once on his Paris rhapsody, he was mistaken, for Alex Aarons and Vinton Freedley prevailed on him to undertake the music for a new musical, *Treasure Girl*. The musical was doomed to failure from the beginning. It had a bad book with a hopelessly silly story of buried treasure found in the last act by Gertrude Lawrence, and though Gershwin produced some moments of excellent music and at least one excellent song, "Feeling I'm Falling," his music could not improve the story. The play folded after sixty-eight performances, with the brokers at their wits' end to sell the tickets. It was still being performed on December 13 when Walter Damrosch conducted the first public performance of *An American in Paris* at Carnegie Hall.

It was another gala evening, with excitement and expectation in the air. For some reason Damrosch had decided to sandwich it between Lekeu's *Adagio for Strings* and the "Fire Scene" from *Die Walküre*. A lengthy summary of the piece, written by Deems Taylor with Gershwin's permission, appeared among the programme notes.

Gershwin's own description was briefer, if less amusing. He

called it "a rhapsodic ballet". He said he had written it very freely and in the most modern style. He was not attempting to portray recognizable Paris scenes. The music was intended to suggest a young American wandering through the streets of Paris, listening to street songs and street music, and finally sitting down in a café, having a couple of drinks and succumbing to nostalgia for the America he has temporarily abandoned. He leaves the café, saunters into the clear air, forgets his nostalgia and listens once again to the triumphant music of the Paris streets.

If that was the purpose, he succeeded magnificently. The jaunty opening bars perfectly convey a spring day in Paris with the chestnut trees in flower. There is a shimmering gaiety in the air. People are talking and going about their affairs without a care in the world. Everywhere there is the hum of excitement—the causeless excitement which affects Parisians in spring as much as it affects foreigners. There are "blue" notes, but these are not to be taken seriously. The American sits down and drinks and gets drunk, and images of past encounters come to him—a bordello, a stately minuet, and somewhere someone is singing a simple song, but the song becomes a solemn high mass, and this in turn gives place to a soaring soprano voice, very sweet—it was probably this passage which caused Vernon Duke, when he was reading the original manuscript, to exclaim, "It is the purest saccharine!"

An American in Paris is not all saccharine, nor is it very pure. There are borrowings everywhere. There is no effort to say anything urgent. Everything is heard and seen in a strange half-waking state in which thoughts and ideas and images coalesce. Noel Coward once wrote a play in which the hero returns drunk to his own apartment, so befuddled that he can hardly see anything in the room which continues to wheel around him. At last the hero believes he can perceive the unity which underlies the apparent chaos of the universe, and says portentously, "Everything merges!" In the same way everything "merges" in *An American in Paris*. Yet somehow, by some magic unknown, Gershwin succeeded in conveying a sense of Paris in the light of innocence, and then in the light of experience. We are made aware of the Garden of Eden, and then of the bleak unhappy children running out through the cold gates. Hidden within the piece there is a morality play.

For *An American in Paris* is not in the least simple and derives from many sources. Gershwin says that it opens "in typical French style, in the manner of Debussy and the Six", but this is nonsense; there is nothing in the least like Debussy in the lilting opening bars or in the ornate confusion of the second movement. This is Gershwin writing on his own nerves, singing of the joys of Paris, but also of the inevitable *cafards*, those periods of haunting depression which affect even the happiest of lovers in Paris and are especially powerful in spring.

But though Gershwin is speaking here more clearly, and far less artificially than in *Rhapsody in Blue*, which can be regarded as a brilliant experiment in bravura, he is also, as often happens in these cases, all the more indebted to others when he is most original. Everywhere there are echoes—of his own songs, of Liszt and Tchaikowsky and even of the posthumous quartets of Beethoven. The church music echoes the *Missa Solemnis*. In fact, almost nothing is original, but the whole is original. No one ever wrote so accurately about Paris seen by an American on a shimmering spring day.

Inevitably there are faults in the piece, which any first-year composition student can point out immediately. There are meaningless bridge passages, many moments when the composer's powers of invention seem to have flagged. Yet the mood is somehow sustained. Joy and Melancholy are seen stripping for the battle, even if they do not engage in war; and the age-old morality play comes to its inevitable conclusion.

When *An American in Paris* was first played in public, the critics tended to pay far too much attention to the strange assortment of instruments with which Gershwin had decorated the piece. Oscar Thompson writing in the *New York Evening Post* declared savagely: "The honks have it. Four automobile horns, vociferously assisted by three saxophones, two tom-toms, rattle, xylophone, wire brush, wood blocks and an ensemble not otherwise innocent of brass or percussion blew or thumped the lid of Carnegie Hall when *An American in Paris* by George Gershwin had its first performance." He went on to ask whether it was conceivable that anyone would remember it in twenty years' time. Herbert Peyser described it as "dull, patchy, thin, vulgar, long-winded, and inane". A more telling criticism came from Paul Rosenfeld who rebuked Gershwin for a quality of opulence which he detected in his music, the same quality which had been noted by Prokofiev. He described the impression produced on him by *An American in Paris*:

> Momentarily we feel the forces of ambition and desire: imperious, unmitigated appetites, yearnings for tenderness, intoxications flowing from the stimulation of novel, luxurious surroundings, Parisian, Cuban, Floridan, from the joy of feeling oneself American—Americanism apparently conceived as a *naïve*, smart, inept, good-natured form of being, happily and humorously shared by other good fellows like oneself—and from a gamin-like eroticism.
>
> It is impossible to hear Gershwin's symphonic music without being from time to time moved by its grandiloquence to conceive—with the aspect of things having some immensely flattering, glorifying bearing upon ourselves—of towers of fine gold arising amid Florida palms, splendiferous hotel foyers crowded with important people and gorgeous women *décolletées jusqu'à là*, and immediately contingent on paradise; or rosy banks of nymphs amorously swooning amid bells of rose-pink tulle.

Paul Rosenfeld's description was true and needed to be said, but it was far from the whole truth. The opulence, the eroticism, the banality, the tawdry smartness were present in the music, as they were present in nearly everything that Gershwin wrote, but they were only a small part of the whole. There was always something of the smart aleck in Gershwin, and it could hardly be otherwise, but this was the least important element in his being. He was in no sense a creator; he was a mirror of his time polished to such a fine degree that he mirrored his age accurately and convincingly, so convincingly indeed that we can look back on *An American in Paris* with a haunting nostalgia, while the music itself reflects the nostalgia of a time we can never recapture.

It was easy in 1928 to laugh at it, and just as easy to understand why it is still being played more than thirty years later. We are no longer alarmed by the taxi horns and most of us have lost any predilection for rosy banks of nymphs, though both are undeniably present in the music. What is important here is a quality which is also present in the painting of Watteau and in some of the passages of the posthumous quartets: there are forms of melancholy and nostalgia so terrible, so much beyond our comprehension and so close to the heartstrings, that they can be suggested only by gaiety. The little dance tunes in the posthumous quartets have power to freeze the blood.

So it was with *An American in Paris*, which is as languorous as a Watteau painting and filled with the same melancholy gaiety. The little dance tunes run on and disappear, like water in sand, and the "blues" are always coming round the next corner. The world is lost for ever, but the dance tune brings it back again; and the girls in the Watteau paintings are tossing in their swings towards an unfathomable blue darkness. Precisely the same mood was caught by F. Scott Fitzgerald in *Tender Is the Night*, and Fitzgerald's work is no less authentic because it describes a society perilously close to the society which embraced Gershwin. When Paul Rosenfeld spoke of Gershwin as "the laureate of music advertisers", he was merely complaining about the cheapness of some of his effects, a complaint which can equally be made against Fitzgerald. Rosenfeld forgot that something of far greater consequence was at stake—the composer was speaking "out of the heart to the heart", and music of this kind has the quality of permanence.

Significantly this was the first large work which Gershwin orchestrated himself. Ferde Grofe had orchestrated the *Rhapsody in Blue*, and to him therefore went much of the credit. Gershwin was determined that this time he should have full control over the work. Henceforth he always orchestrated his major works.

Paul Rosenfeld was not alone in detecting a failure of nerve in *An American in Paris*. Even Gershwin's friends and close admirers were troubled by some aspects of his talent. His unnerving pride could be tolerated, for his talent was prodigious. What was lacking was compassion, the sense of the human condition. At a party given by Jules Glaenzer on the night of the première Otto Kahn made a little speech more than hinting that it was time Gershwin descended from the clouds. He said:

> Far be it from me to wish any tragedy to come into the life of this nation for the sake of chastening its soul, or into the life of George Gershwin for the sake of deepening his art.
> But I do wish to quote to him a few verses (by Thomas

Hardy, I believe) which I came across the other day and which are supposed to relate to America:

> *I shrink to see a modern coast*
> *Whose riper times have yet to be;*
> *Where the new regions claim them free*
> *From that long drip of human tears*
> *Which people old in tragedy*
> *Have left upon the centuried years.*

"The long drip of human tears," my dear George! They have great and strange and beautiful power, those human tears. They fertilize the deepest roots of art, and from them spring flowers of a loveliness and perfume that no other moisture can produce.

I believe in you with full faith and admiration—in your personality, your gifts, your art, your future, your significance in the field of American music, and I wish you well with all my heart. And just because of that, I could wish for you an experience, not too prolonged, of that driving storm and stress of the emotions, of your solitary wrestling with your soul, of that aloofness, for a while, from the actions and distractions of the everyday world, which are the most effective ingredients for the deepening and mellowing and complete development, the energizing and revealment of an artist's inner being and spiritual powers.

It was a good speech: very warm, penetrating, to the point. He was saying with authority what needed to be said at exactly the right moment, and Gershwin seems to have taken the lesson to heart without ever knowing how to put it into effect. "The long drip of human tears" appears momentarily in *Porgy and Bess*. It appears nowhere else. The truth was that he had very little compassion, very little tolerance and understanding of other people, and very little natural generosity: yet he could be kind and helpful to his fellow composers, advancing their work wherever possible. His enthusiasms were centred upon himself.

Long afterwards when he was dead and his disturbing memory was still being held in great honour, Oscar Levant wrote bitterly, "The trouble was that he seemed to be writing for the five thousand people who went to the Lido, knew the best clubs in

London, and thought Elsa Maxwell a leader in society. There were flaws everywhere." Gershwin seems to have been well aware of the flaws, but unable to do very much about them. He could not make war against himself, against the *chutzpah* which had been bred into him on the East Side. To be facile and accomplished, to produce second-rate works of art with extraordinary technical virtuosity—this he could do at any time; but to produce a great work of art which would enlarge experience and enhance life, providing lasting exhilaration to his audience—this had escaped him. There was the *Rhapsody in Blue*, the *Concerto in F* and *An American in Paris*—these, whatever their faults, were authentic works of art, yet of a minor character. In the few short years that remained he was to produce one major work and a good deal of charming nonsense.

It is difficult to understand why he chose the easy road when there were so many tantalizing opportunities for writing compositions of lasting importance. The closest of his friends implored him to concentrate on work which was worthy of him. He had no need to write film music and musical comedies: there was enough money in the bank. He was like an iron filing caught up in all the magnetic forces of his time, tossed hither and thither, never knowing where he was going, hoping in some strange way that he could be at once a social lion, a concert performer, a dilettante, an accomplished painter and a composer with a range extending from classical music to honky-tonk.

On the night of the première of *An American in Paris*, his friends decided to give him a present in commemoration of the event. They were considerably exercised about what to give him, and at last settled on a gleaming brass humidor which would keep his cigars fresh—those cigars which he always smoked at a jaunty angle. It was as though his friends were bowing before the image he had created of himself—eternally young, eternally jaunty, with no serious thought in the world.

7

The Wasted Years

ON THE RARE occasions when Gershwin talked about the past, he would remember one of the innumerable railroad flats and tenements presided over by his mother, who spent much of her life in the kitchen, a woman who was always calm amid the tornado of the East Side, unlike the shiftless father who was curiously excitable and often frightened by poverty. He would remember the dreariness of those ill-furnished apartments, the clatter of the elevated railway, the warfare in the streets. He was glad he had escaped from them.

His father never completely escaped from them. There was something faintly pathetic about this man, who smoked cheap cigars and carried himself with the air of a bank president, even when his affairs were in a state of chaos. He was a showman, and never took life seriously. He was like a guest in his own house, not rejected by his family, but never quite belonging to it. Rose was made of different stuff—the family revolved around her. In Gershwin's eyes she was rich in all the graces of charity and kindness. "She's what the mammy writers write about, and what the mammy singers sing about," Gershwin said of her. "But they don't mean it, and I do!"

Morris Gershwin found his greatest happiness in amusing the children. He liked singing to them, and he was even better at whistling. He had no great musical gifts, but he could coax music out of anything—combs, clothespins, pencils, paper clips and rubber bands. He could play a cornet to perfection, without a cornet. He went to the Jewish opera, remembered the tunes and sang them about the house. In later years, when George was famous, he liked to sit outside his son's door and listen to the endless improvisations out of which songs would grow, a dazed smile on his face. He would become restless if there were long pauses. On one famous occasion, when Gershwin had been silent for all of five minutes, his father burst into the room and said excitedly, "Can I help, George? You got up to here——" And he began to whistle some bars that Gershwin had been playing before the fit of silence overcame him.

George Gershwin was the son of Morris and Rose, and much more like his father than he ever acknowledged. He was shiftless like his father, and he had his father's charm, and his father's love of easy money. "My father coaxed music out of the silliest contraptions," Gershwin remarked once, referring to the clothespins and the combs; and that instinct for making music out of whatever implements were at hand was inherited by the son, who used taxi horns, wood-blocks, tom-toms and rattles in *An American in Paris*; and he would have gone on to use even more obscure instruments if they had been available.

In almost every way Gershwin betrayed the influence of his father. In him the image was sharpened, refined, brought into focus. Like his father, he was trapped by his own facility and could turn his energies in any direction he pleased, without bothering whether they were worth-while.

His first task after *An American in Paris* was to write the songs for a Ziegfeld musical comedy called *Show Girl*, starring Ruby Keeler. It was perhaps the worst show that Ziegfeld ever produced. It was loud and vulgar and silly, and pleased no one, in spite of an impressive array of talents, which included Jimmy Durante, Eddie Foy and the Duke Ellington Band. Inevitably there was a ballet based on *An American in Paris*. Jimmy Durante sang his own night-club songs, and Ruby Keeler sang "Liza". On at least three occasions her husband Al Jolson popped up in the stalls and sang the refrain to his wife. There were good lyrics by Ira Gershwin and Gus Kahn, but the entire production had something of the appearance of warmed-over toast and was soon withdrawn. It was Ziegfeld's most spectacular flop, and since he was inclined to blame everyone except himself, there were endless recriminations. Ziegfeld's fury was unbounded. He refused to pay royalties to Gershwin, and the case was fought through the courts. Gershwin won. It was not his fault that the musical was a calamitous failure, but he was wildly at fault in permitting himself to take part in it.

Gershwin was still committed to Broadway, still saw himself as the composer of an endless series of musical comedies. *Strike up the Band!*, written in 1927 and then abandoned, was suddenly revived, with a new libretto largely written by Morrie Ryskind and with some new songs composed by Gershwin. It was one more musical comedy to add to the growing list, but it had the merit of some acid comments on war, although at the time war was not a very pressing fact of human existence. Horace J. Fletcher, a chocolate manufacturer with a penchant for using Grade B milk, invades Switzerland when Washington refuses to raise the tariff on chocolate. He destroys the enemy and returns in triumph. His triumph, however, is short-lived, for it is soon discovered that he has been adulterating his chocolate bars, and he gains nothing from his adventure.

But while Horace J. Fletcher gained nothing, the audience gained a good deal of witty verse and a vast amount of light-hearted music. Tariffs and pacifism and even the war against Switzerland were merely devices for bringing the actors on the stage. The theme song mimicked a military march to perfection, and earned the special blessing of William Bolitho, who wrote an entire essay on the song. "Of all things in the world," he wrote, "here is a bitter, rather good satirical attack on war, genuine propaganda at times, sung and danced on Broadway to standing room only." *Rather good;* not *very good*. His enthusiasm was tempered by the knowledge that in the end it amounted to very little, and the really surprising thing was that a comedy with a faintly discernible anti-war theme was playing at all. In the history of musical comedies and operettas it must rank with Offenbach's *La Duchesse de Gerolstein*, and it seems to have sprung from the same causes. America in the last months before the depression had much in common with France in the last years of Napoleon III.

Like *La Duchesse de Gerolstein, Strike up the Band!* had the merit of unwavering lightheartedness. There was no real plot. The war, in the final version presented on Broadway, took place only in Horace J. Fletcher's dreams. There were songs like "I've Got a Crush on You" and "I'm a Typical Self-Made American", and these were sung and hummed long after the play closed. More important was Gershwin's growing command of orchestration and his determination to break through the commonplace forms of musical comedy and introduce music with more weight and significance. Here and there were passages of music which sounded worthy of the composer of *An American in Paris*, and although there were not many of these passages, there were enough to suggest that he was still experimenting and increasing his range of expression.

Gershwin was delighted with *Strike up the Band!* and came to regard it as the best of his musical comedies up to this time. On opening night he jumped down into the orchestra pit and performed as conductor, waving his baton briskly and singing the songs in his small voice to such effect that one reviewer pointedly asked whether he was not the star of the show.

As a conductor of his own works he was in his element, and he was enjoying an increasing experience of the conductor's rôle. Any challenge excited him, and just as he had determined to be the best orchestrator of his own works, so he determined to be the best conductor. On August 26, 1929, nearly six months before the opening of *Strike up the Band!*, he had appeared as guest conductor and soloist in Lewisohn Stadium. He conducted *An American in Paris*. He was almost delirious with pleasure and enthusiasm. The stadium was crowded to capacity. He took his bows under the white shell which enclosed the orchestra, and decided to conduct his works at every opportunity. In November he conducted *An American in Paris* again with the Manhattan Symphony Orchestra, with the same success.

He loved conducting, but possessed none of the traditional conductor's accomplishments. He had almost no capacity to read a score, and in addition he had a bad musical memory, except of his own works. He learned to conduct by listening to phonograph records of his music and beating time in front of a mirror. Singing helped him; and he sang through nearly all these performances.

He was at the height of his fame, and from every corner demands were being made for his services. He was "hot" in Tin Pan Alley, and equally "hot" in Lewisohn Stadium and Carnegie Hall. He had no rivals, or none that he regarded as rivals. If there had been any legitimate rivals in sight, he might have devoted more of his time to "classical" music. In fact he spent the next years writing music for films and musical comedies, dispersing his talents, and often wasting his energies, trapped by his own facility.

For Vinton Freedley he wrote the music for *Girl Crazy* to the book by Guy Bolton and Jack MacGowan. It is remembered as a frothy musical comedy, with a silly plot about a dude ranch for Broadway chorus girls, chiefly distinguished by Gershwin's songs, which were among the best he ever wrote. The star was Ginger Rogers, who received fifteen hundred dollars a week, at that time a stupendous sum for a Broadway actress. Ethel Merman, making her debut on the musical comedy stage, received three hundred and seventy-five dollars a week. This was a little unfair, since Ethel Merman brought down the house every night with her rendering of "I've Got Rhythm". She played the part of Kate Fothergill the wife of the man who ran the gambling room in the dude ranch, while Ginger Rogers played Molly, the postmistress at Custerville, Arizona. It was Ethel Merman's play. At five minutes to ten, wearing a black satin skirt, a low-cut red blouse and bangles up her arms, she sang "Sam and Delilah", a western dance-hall torch song, and stopped the play. Ten minutes later, leaning casually against the proscenium arch again, she stopped the play for the second time with another song. She very nearly stopped the play for the third time when she sang "Boy, What Love Has Done To Me". Ginger Rogers sang "Embraceable You" to Allen Kearns, who sang the playboy rôle in the play; but it was Ethel Merman, fresh from the night-clubs and obscure theatrical engagements, who set all the bells ringing.

Ethel Merman made *Girl Crazy*. She belted out the songs, but she had grace and charm. There was no Broadway glitter about her, but she performed like someone who had spent her life on Broadway. She was strangely modest, and in her presence Gershwin showed more than his usual degree of modesty. He invited her to his apartment on Riverside Drive, played "I Got Rhythm" to her on the piano, and asked her whether there was anything she would like changed. Too dumbfounded to reply, she waited until he asked the question again, and then piped, "It will do very nicely, Mr. Gershwin." It did very nicely indeed, and there were people who went to see *Girl Crazy* for no other reason except to hear her sing that song.

Ethel Merman was a prodigy, and unlike most prodigies, she was totally devoid of complexes. Off-stage she was singularly quiet and even-tempered, the result perhaps of her Baptist upbringing. After her performance a drama critic announced that "she approaches sex in song with the cold fury of a philosopher. She aims at a point slightly above the entrails, but knocks you out all the same." It would be more true to say that she sang out of sheer uncomplicated *joie de vivre*. Gershwin, who was complex and inclined to bend to every wind, regarded her with awe. On the day after the first performance he invited her to lunch and asked her whether she had read the reviews, all of them extolling her to the skies. She had not bothered to read them, and he was more awestruck than ever. Gershwin read all his reviews, to the very last word and the very last page, and he was hurt by the slightest criticism. When Gershwin and Ethel Merman met, the naked nerve met perfect serenity, and he very rarely met it again.

Since everything Gershwin touched turned to gold, it was inevitable that he should go to Hollywood. He had neither the strength nor the native intelligence to resist that savage and powerful force; and none of his close friends were in any position to dissuade him from following his own inclinations. *Girl Crazy* opened on October 14, 1930, with Gershwin conducting: two weeks later he was on his way to the West Coast to write the score for a Fox musical comedy film called *Delicious*, no better and no worse than a hundred other musical comedies on film, with a silly story of a Scots girl meeting a wealthy New Yorker on shipboard and wrapping him round her fingers. It was easy work. It took only seven weeks, and there were long golfing holidays in Palm Springs. It was his first visit to California.

Gershwin enjoyed the tempo of life in California, the long hours of hard work followed by arduous and exhausting play. He enjoyed the hard sunlight and the presence of beautiful women. His fame was at least as great as that of the most famous musical comedy star, and he enjoyed being famous among the famous.

He still did some serious work. A short orchestral sequence from *Delicious* was extracted bodily from the film and made to serve as the basis for a short orchestral sequence intended to convey the feeling of New York under the shattering impact of the riveters at work among the skyscrapers—the rhythms of riveting were introduced into the music. He worked on this rhapsody in Hollywood and later in New York. The composition was completed in May; in June he hired a fifty-six man orchestra in the NBC studios and conducted a special private performance which was recorded. He then studied and restudied the records for weeks. He was a musician who played by ear and learned by ear, and this rather devious method of composition was in fact a very sensitive one, given his peculiar limitations.

This composition continually changed its name. At various times it was known as the *Rhapsody in Rivets*, *Manhattan Rhapsody*, the *New York Rhapsody*, until finally it became the *Second Rhapsody* in imitation of Liszt's *Second Hungarian Rhapsody*, for which Gershwin possessed unbounded admiration. The shadow of Liszt falls over his entire work.

The *Second Rhapsody* is a rather shattering experience, and entirely unlike the *Rhapsody in Blue*. Most of the Gershwin themes are memorable because they are designed on simple melodic patterns, but there is very little that is memorable in the *Second Rhapsody*, in spite of its brilliant "blues" passages. Gershwin scored it for full orchestra and took care to introduce as many novel instruments as possible, including fly swatters and wood blocks. The first performance was given by the Boston Symphony Orchestra with Serge Koussevitsky conducting on January 29, 1932. Gershwin was the piano soloist. The reviews troubled him. The *Boston Evening Transcript* said, "It sounded over-often from the study table and the piano rack," but gave him credit for skill and invention. There was a warning note—"Mr. Gershwin waxes in craftsmanship but at the cost of earlier and irresistible *élan*." The *Second Rhapsody* received better notices in New York, but there was a widespread feeling that it represented a sterile phase of his development. It is no longer regarded as belonging to the canon of Gershwin's major musical works.

Rhumba, which he wrote in the following year, fared better. It owed its origin to a brief holiday in Cuba early in 1932. A short work, it is among the most charming and least pretentious of his orchestral compositions, and gives the impression of being tossed off during a few weeks in which he was intoxicated with Cuban rhythms. It was, in fact, written in three weeks. Gershwin had a special fondness for the piece, which was given its première at Lewisohn Stadium on August 16, 1932, only a week after he had completed the orchestration. For the first time an all-Gershwin programme was being offered, and he was wildly excited when he learned that the all-time attendance had been broken on the night of the performance.

Rhumba deserves attention because it displays nearly all the virtues and vices of Gershwin's minor work. That "irresistible *élan*", of which the *Boston Evening Transcript* had spoken, is in full evidence. There are the inevitable abrupt changes of mood, the inevitable clarinet cadenzas introducing the "blues" passages, and the inevitable thickly embroidered orchestration. It is "schmaltzy", but not too "schmaltzy". It starts to the same beat as *An American in Paris*, and it is possible to read into it a description of a Cuban fiesta as seen and enjoyed by an American wandering by accident into Havana. It echoes *An American in Paris* even to the extent of introducing passages of quiet and purposeless meditation: it is perfectly possible to imagine an American sitting down at a café after being deafened by the fiesta and then slowly getting maudlin drunk, only to be awakened sharply by the resounding concluding passages, which form an imperious salute to the Iberian heritage.

Though *Rhumba* is a minor extravaganza, Gershwin was inclined to take it seriously. Later he gave it the title *Cuban Overture*, explaining that such a title "gives a more just idea of the character and intent of the music".

Rhumba is essentially lighthearted music without any attempt to dive below the surface of things. His music for *Of Thee I Sing* belonged to a different order altogether. It is the best of his musical comedies, the most irreverent, and the most mature. For the first time he employed all his available musical artifices to underscore the action. The play was a hilarious spoof on the Presidency with no holds barred, and the music was designed to take every possible advantage of the satirical plot, which involved the attempts of the superbly mythical John P. Wintergreen to enter the White House. *Strike up the Band!* was a parody of war and big business. *Of Thee I Sing* was a parody of Washington and all forms of elective government; and had a sharper sting in its tail.

Of Thee I Sing told the story of John P. Wintergreen's campaign for the Presidency with enough semblance of truth to make it almost convincing. According to the book, which was sketched out by George Kaufman and Morrie Ryskind in a few days in Atlantic City, John P. Wintergreen is one of those brilliantly colourless politicians who are provided with their electoral programmes by their political agents; and since none of the conventional programmes suited him, it was decided to launch him on a programme of LOVE. But even in a lovesick land, Wintergreen as "the Great Emancipator" carries little weight. There must be a gimmick. Accordingly a beauty contest is arranged in Atlantic City to elect "Miss White House". She is duly elected in the person of Diana Devereaux, a luscious Southern *belle*, and the election agents quite properly plan to carry them together into the White House.

This is all very well, and Wintergreen is perfectly prepared to share their enthusiasm for the Southern *belle* until at the last moment he spies his old-fashioned secretary and promptly marries her because she can bake corn muffins. Wintergreen and the little secretary become the President and First Lady.

Meanwhile Miss Devereaux, with the massed assistance of all the Southern Senators, proceeds to claim her rightful inheritance. When she learns that she is "the illegitimate daughter of an illegitimate son of an illegitimate nephew of Napoleon", it occurs to her that there are advantages in illegitimacy, and the French Ambassador intervenes on her behalf, threatening to break off diplomatic relations. The mouselike secretary, who has become the First Lady, chooses this moment to announce to the Senate that she has just become a mother. The Senators are overcome, jump to their feet and rock imaginary babies in their arms. Miss Devereaux is still on the warpath. The President is about to be impeached when it is decided to offer Miss Devereaux to the Vice-President in order to pacify the French.

The Vice-President, Alexander Throttlebottom, is even more colourless than the President. There is nothing to be said in his favour except that he is charmingly vague on all subjects including the Vice-Presidency. No one knows him; no one will *ever* know him. He cannot even get a ticket for the Public Library in Washington because he cannot find two references, and when he at last enters the White House, it is only because he has joined a tour of sightseers. Acted by Victor Moore, he emerged as a creature of infinite comic pathos.

The Vice-President very nearly stole the show. Lois Moran took the part of the secretary, and William Gaxton played Wintergreen with exactly the right shade of meaningless aplomb. It was one of those rare musicals where the details were subordinate to the whole; and the performance went with a rush, the audience never having time to catch its breath. John Mason Brown described it as "an audacious clowning of the sentimentality of our people and the means of our politics which, with no reverence but much good humour, pokes fun at our campaign strategy, invades both the sacrosanct Senate Chamber and the White

House, and chucks the august members of our Supreme Court playfully under their bewhiskered chins".

But if John Mason Brown was suggesting that it was hardly more than a happy spoof, he was wrong. There was much deliberate irreverence, and many sharp things were said sharply. George Kaufman and Morrie Ryskind had written a light-hearted and implausible comedy, which derived bite and resonance from the music. While *Strike up the Band!* hurt no one, *Of Thee I Sing* struck at the general complacency of the nation. It was hilariously funny, and also strangely moving. Those who hoped that Gershwin would help to create the American equivalent of the Gilbert and Sullivan operetta were now rewarded.

To nearly everyone's surprise the authors of the book were awarded the Pulitzer Prize. No prize was given to the composer, perhaps because the Pulitzer Prize committee could not bring themselves to regard the music as "best representing the emotional value and power of the stage". Yet the music was more than half the play. Gershwin was not particularly annoyed by the oversight, and it pleased him that Ira, who wrote the lyrics, received a cheque for $333.33 and an embossed and sealed certificate from the Trustees of Columbia University.

Of Thee I Sing was, quite properly, the most successful of all Gershwin's musical comedies, running for 441 performances. *Let 'Em Eat Cake*, which followed, was a terrible failure. It purported to be a musical comedy with a social message. John P. Wintergreen and Alexander Throttlebottom return to the scene. Defeated in the election Wintergreen leads a left-wing revolution, organizes a blue-shirt army, and brings about a dictatorship of the proletariat. Throttlebottom is condemned to the guillotine, which is set up in Union Square. Fascism and Communism are hilariously attacked, but the attack is curiously unconvincing. The rousing song, "Comes the Revolution" may have been written with excellent intentions, but it had no relation to the spirit of the times. The wretched musical faltered through a hundred performances on Broadway, and then collapsed.

Let 'Em Eat Cake was an experiment in social drama, an attempt to leap across the interval which separated musical comedy from the lives of ordinary people caught up in the misery of the Depression. It tried to say something of importance, and failed because the authors had nothing important to say.

Five days after it opened Gershwin signed a contract with the Theatre Guild which gave him the musical rights to the play *Porgy*, written by DuBose and Dorothy Heyward, which he had long admired. Now at long last, with a superb play to work with, he was able to say important things in an important way.

8

Porgy and Bess

IT ALL BEGAN with a crippled Negro called Samuel Smalls, who went about Charleston in a goat cart and had the reputation of creating trouble with women. He was a Congo Negro, purple-black, with a frail body and heavy hands, and a curious habit of meditation which permitted him to gaze for long periods fixedly ahead, while he waited for the money to fall into his tin cup. He had a police record, and was in and out of jails. One day, in the early twenties, the Charleston *News and Courier* had a small paragraph on the back page about his latest crime: "Samuel Smalls, who is a cripple and familiar to King Street with his goat and cart, was held for the June term of court of sessions on an aggravated assault charge. It is alleged that on Saturday night he attempted to shoot Maggie Barnes." Samuel Smalls disappeared into the city jail and nothing else was ever heard of him except that shortly afterwards a body bearing a tag inscribed with his name was buried on James Island, off the Carolina coast.

So Samuel Smalls passed into history, and it could never have occurred to him that he would become a folk legend of towering proportions. "Goat Sammy," the gnarled Negro with the thatch of greying hair and the angry bloodshot eyes, riding in a soap-box on wheels tethered to an evil-smelling goat, has no more claim to our sympathy than Billy the Kid. He was dangerous and disreputable, and more than half-mad. Many women had cause to regret his existence, and the police were weary of arresting him. He was a useless member of society and a public nuisance.

He became a folk hero as the result of a long and complex chain of events, beginning when the young novelist DuBose Heyward began to write his first novel at the MacDowell Colony in New Hampshire the summer after he married. One day his eyes had fallen on the paragraph in the *News and Courier*; it brought back to him a flood of memories about that strange impassive Negro. He decided to write about Samuel Smalls. In a sense it would be a factual novel, about a real man in a real place at a real time, and for no particular reason he chose the time around 1912. He had himself suffered from a crippling attack of polio when he was seventeen, and accordingly he felt for "Goat Sammy" an extraordinary sympathy and a curious revulsion. All his intellectual energy, all his understanding of the Negroes and all his talent as a writer would be placed at the service of "Goat Sammy".

As the novel progressed, he found it necessary to change very little. His people were real people, as he knew them. Long ago Cabbage Row was an elegant mansion, the four sides of the mansion forming a great courtyard, but now it was falling into ruin, and was given over to Negro tenements. He changed Cabbage Row to Catfish Row, and he changed "Goat Sammy" to Porgo. He wrote half the novel, and sent it to Harcourt, Brace, the publishers, who immediately rejected it on the grounds that they were not accustomed to considering half-finished novels. Later the novel fell into the hands of John Farrar, who had the good sense to snap up the novel immediately. Farrar's judgement was vindicated, for the book has become a minor classic.

Almost at the very last minute DuBose Heyward changed the name of his chief character. Porgo became Porgy, and the legend had begun.

Porgy, larger than life, was to grow until he assumed fantastic dimensions. His desperate love for Bess was to be celebrated across the nation. He was to be remembered in countries where Charleston was never heard of. In book, in song, on the stage, on wide-screen film in blazing colour he was to be celebrated as no Negro, not even Uncle Tom, was celebrated; and it is not surprising that many Negroes objected violently.

The Negroes objected for many reasons. DuBose Heyward was a Southerner with some of the prejudices of the South. His attitude towards the Negroes was complex, gentle and violent by turns. He was torn between admiration for their beauty and joyful acceptance of life, and their poverty and acceptance of poverty. He was fascinated by their violence: the novel is full of an aching respect for the primitive instinctual life of the senses. He knew the Negroes well. He came from old plantation stock, he had run an insurance business in Charleston and been a cotton checker on the waterfront. In his early poems he had attempted to speak with

Negro intonations, and he possessed an extensive knowledge of Negro dialects. But he could not write about Negroes calmly and dispassionately; he loved them desperately and was horrified by them, and all through *Porgy* there is evidence of the civil war he fought within himself, for mastery over his own feelings about the Negroes.

He wrote the book with difficulty, with many false starts, never quite clear until the end where he was going, chipping it off his breastbone all through the spring, summer and fall of 1924. He wrote to friends about his doubts and hesitations. Would the public—especially the public of Charleston—accept a book which was about Negroes? He was an American aristocrat, descended from the famous Thomas Heyward who had signed the Declaration of Independence, and what on earth was he doing writing about the simple Negroes who lived between Cabbage Row and Vanderhorst's Wharf?

Much of the strength of the novel springs from the compulsive war he fought with himself to bring the novel into existence. There is nothing lovable or gentle in the characters he invented: they are stark, almost animal-like, larger than life. Their passions are elemental, and they suffer from inexplicable rages which flare unaccountably and senselessly. He saw Bess as a tall gaunt tragic figure, like many of those middle-aged Negro women he had seen on the Charleston waterfront, with an ugly scar on her left cheek and the hard lines about her mouth etched with the acid of utter degradation. In time she was to become a voluptuous young woman, but that was not the fault of the novelist, who painted her in the sombre colours of disease and drunkenness.

Nor was there anything in the least like a romantic hero in Porgy, old before his time, possessing the patience of the animals, at once full-lipped and hard-mouthed, with no other aim in life except a sullen determination to survive. He lives on the edge of consciousness, and when we see him first he is "waiting with the concentrating energy of a burning-glass", but he never knows what he is waiting for. Only Crown has heroic stature with his springing thighs straining his cotton pants, his slender waist and his handsome torso. "Wid uh body like dat," says Maria, "why yuh is goin' aroun' huntin' fuh deat'?" In fact all the Negroes in the novel are hunting after death. Death is everywhere—in the dead Crown, in the wheeling buzzards, in the ships that crash against the wharf during a storm, and in the figure of Maria who is last seen with a cleaver in her hands, a widening pool of blood at her feet, while she carves up the carcass of a shark.

Death, then, is the main theme of the novel—death in its turbulence and savagery. The Negroes are frightened by it, cannot understand it, and since they can have no recourse to the white man's science or the white man's God, they must depend upon the power of the ancient tribal symbols and "the presciences that shuddered like dawn at the back of the brain". But those powers cannot help them. In the end they are alone. They have nowhere to go and nothing to fall back on. When the hurricane sweeps through Catfish Row, DuBose Heyward describes the havoc, and concludes: "The ruin was utter." He might well have said the same about the fate of his characters.

Utter ruin faces Porgy when Bess leaves him. In the novel as it was printed, we see him sitting alone with his goat, stunned by the blow, unable to move or think, gazing up into "an irony of summer sunlight". In an earlier version he simply vanishes from the earth—"Porgo had gone where no one knew—where shadows go in twilight, where the morning stars go in the crucible of day." Porgy's famous flight to New York in search of Bess was an afterthought, introduced into the play which came two years later.

Porgy, published in 1925, was an immediate success, as it deserved to be. DuBose Heyward had said elemental things in an elemental prose, and no one had written quite like this since the time of Melville. He told a horrifyingly tragic story, and all the best stories are horrifyingly tragic. But Porgy, stunned, helpless and embittered, with his goat and his soap-box, was only beginning his life on earth.

DuBose Heyward had the good fortune to marry a brilliant dramatist, who set about transforming the novel into a play. In the process many subtle transformations took place. Some of the horror vanished. Interludes of comedy were introduced. The white men who played a minor rôle in the novel were developed, and the Negro lawyer Simon Frasier, who sells illegal certificates of divorce to the Negroes, almost became a major character. Music was added in the form of spirituals and choruses; and the music, though urgent and wonderfully effective, had the effect of drowning the tragedy. As the curtain falls, Porgy is about to

Porgy and Bess at the Alvin Theatre, New York, October 1935

(*Above*) Todd Duncan, Anne Brown and John W. Bubbles in *Porgy and Bess*, 1935

(*Left*) George Gershwin in the middle 'thirties

leave for New York, in the hope of finding his beloved Bess, who was played by a young Negro actress of astonishing beauty.

The play was as successful as the book, with a run of 367 performances in New York.

Gershwin attended one of the performances and met the authors. He was excited by the operatic possibilities of the play and spoke about writing music for an operatic version. It was a brief meeting; no promises were made; and soon afterwards he went off on his extended tour of Europe which produced *An American in Paris*. He seems to have forgotten the play, or at least to have put it at the back of his mind, until one day in March, 1932, on the eve of another journey abroad, he wrote to DuBose Heyward, reminding him of their conversation almost exactly four years before and saying that he was thinking of setting it to music. "It is still the most outstanding play that I know about coloured people," he wrote.

Then once more he seems to have forgotten *Porgy*. There was a brief exchange of correspondence, followed by silence. In the following year DuBose Heyward, who was then in New York, called him to say that the Theatre Guild, which had put on the original production, was asking for permission to let Jerome Kern and Oscar Hammerstein II produce *Porgy* as a musical, with Al Jolson in the leading rôle. Negotiations were far advanced. Al Jolson was at the height of his fame, and the recent Kern and Hammerstein production of *Show Boat*, based on the Edna Ferber novel, had been a wildfire success. DuBose Heyward was in no position to refuse the offer of the Theatre Guild, which had loyally come to his aid when he was hoping to find a producer for the original production of *Porgy*. At the same time he had no illusions about the kind of musical comedy which might result if it was placed in the hands of Kern and Hammerstein with their preference for using white men in Negro roles. Heyward had lost money in the stock market crash of 1929. He was not rich and needed any money he could get, but he was prepared to hold out if Gershwin would write the score and help him to transform the play into a memorable folk opera.

At the time Gershwin was committed to writing *Let 'Em Eat Cake*, but he promised to spend every available minute on *Porgy*. From now on he was dedicated to the project. In October of that year a formal contract was drawn up, and the work began.

It was slow work, for both Heyward and Gershwin were determined to produce an authentic opera which would rival the great German and Italian operas. It was to be called *Porgy and Bess*, on the model of *Tristan und Isolde*. Heyward was to write the libretto. Neither Heyward nor Gershwin had ever before worked on a full-length opera.

From the beginning things went surprisingly well. Heyward, the aristocratic Southerner, was deeply impressed by the modesty and vitality of the born-and-bred New Yorker. He described Gershwin as "a young man of enormous physical and emotional vitality, who possessed the faculty of seeing himself quite impersonally and realistically, and who knew exactly what he wanted and where he was going". Gershwin in turn was favourably impressed by Heyward's charm and his capacity for hard work. In almost everything they were opposites. Heyward lacked facility; he was cautious; he possessed a genuine modesty; and he suffered from paralysing spells of doubt over his own creativity.

To Heyward, Gershwin showed the best side of his character. Rarely humble, he showed a surprising humility, nearly always deferring to Heyward's judgement. There were none of the seething quarrels which often plague librettists and composers. Much of the time they worked at a distance of a thousand miles, with Heyward in South Carolina and Gershwin in New York exchanging their ideas through the mails. There were brief visits. Gershwin went down to Charleston for a few days in January 1934, and Heyward stayed for a few days in Gershwin's New York apartment in April. By this time most of Act One and Act Two had been sketched out. Ira's role was to be the catalytic agent, the quiet and seemingly inactive partner in the enterprise, pushing it forward without ever appearing to do so. He sometimes sharpened Heyward's lyrics and maintained a kind of overall supervision. Heyward was fascinated by the way the brothers would take hold of a lyric, and then "after their extraordinary fashion they would get at the piano, pound, wrangle, swear, burst into weird snatches of song, and eventually emerge with a polished lyric".

Inevitably there were minor disagreements. Heyward wanted the dialogue to be spoken: Gershwin wanted recitative. Heyward pointed out that the story had to keep moving and that they could ill afford the time for recitative, and there were already enough choruses and genre scenes to hold up the action. Gershwin replied that opera had always employed recitative and he saw no reason to change the conventional pattern. In the end, of course, there was far too much recitative and a good deal of it had to be cut out, with the result that the opera became largely a succession of songs and choruses. "Bess, you is my woman now" is one line in the play. In the opera it covers nine pages of song.

By the summer nearly the whole of the libretto had been sketched out, much of it in great detail, and Gershwin was already beginning to see it as a whole. He felt, however, that something was missing. He knew the sophisticated New York Negroes, but not the primitive Negroes of the South. Accordingly he decided to spend two months of the summer in South Carolina, soaking up atmosphere and listening to spirituals. A cottage at Folly Beach, a small island ten miles off Charleston, was rented for him. It was a small frame structure with almost no furniture, no drinking water laid on—it came in five-gallon crocks from Charleston every day—and only the most primitive sanitary facilities. It threatened to fall with the first storm, like some of the other cottages on the beach which disintegrated during a storm a few days before Gershwin arrived with his cousin Henry Botkin, who brought his painting equipment and set out to paint the Negroes. Gershwin did a little painting, but he was determined to work on the opera. In those eight weeks he worked as he had rarely worked before.

He had lived in luxury; now he was living in satisfying poverty. His workroom was his bedroom, with an imported upright piano beside the bed, which was usually unmade. There was a single naked electric lamp hanging over the bed, and the only decoration to the room consisted of the metronome which ticked away relentlessly on the top of the piano. Sand crabs crawled across the plain board floor; crickets chirped all night; flies, gnats, and mosquitoes made the air hideous. Gershwin and Botkin wandered around in bathing suits, unshaved, dirty, and supremely happy. Gershwin even grew a beard.

Heyward developed the theory that this visit was "a homecoming". In some indefinable way Gershwin's apartment in New York, with its Japanese screens and air of abandoned luxury, was wrong. It was like a stage setting, unreal, flashy, almost the caricature of the apartment of a rising young musician. At Folly

Beach he was living down to earth. No superbly appointed bathrooms: only a nail on the wall from which he hung his clothes, and a chipped wash basin for bathing. The heat came out of the sky, and the damp came from the sea. One could imagine a poverty-stricken Jewish musician in New York's East Side living in a similar dilapidated apartment.

Heyward's theory went further. For him Gershwin was never so alive, so sensitive to all that happened around him, or so brilliantly in command of his own music as during the weeks he spent at Folly Beach or during the brief visits he paid to the Heywards' house at Hendersonville in North Carolina. In the South he was like a man who had found himself, glowing with physical vitality and spiritual health. A group of Gullah Negroes shuffling along a dusty road or lifting their voices in spirituals produced in him a kind of ecstasy, an almost terrifying sense of communion. He seemed to step out of himself, to become someone else altogether.

One day at Hendersonville they were about to enter a rundown cabin used by Negro Holy Rollers when Gershwin suddenly held Heyward by the arm. He did not want to go in. He wanted to stand in the open, enjoying the astonishing music that poured out—a music compounded of many different rhythms, all of them complex, yet fusing together into a single pounding rhythm of barbaric intensity. Perhaps twelve people were singing inside, but it sounded like a full orchestra. The voices and the words were lost, but there was the sense of many rhythms forming a clearly defined pattern of remarkable power. The Negroes were invoking their God with a fierce primitive abandon. This was music "at the heart of things", as far removed as possible from the superficial gaiety of so much of Gershwin's music. He was spellbound. Months later when he came to write the music for the hurricane scene in *Porgy and Bess*, he deliberately tried to recreate the mood of the strange chanting he had heard outside the Negro church at Hendersonville with six different prayers sung simultaneously.

On another occasion Heyward introduced him to the "shouting" of the Gullah Negroes. "Shouting" also had its origins in Africa. It was chanting accompanied by a complex rhythmic pattern beaten out by the clapping of hands and the stamping of feet. The Negroes whirled about. They tossed their arms jerkily.

They abandoned themselves to powerful rhythms, which appeared at first to belong to no recognizable pattern. It was as though some very strange and long-forgotten ceremony was being performed by people who were almost out of their senses with the terror and agony of worship; and they went on, endlessly clapping and stamping and shouting as though time had vanished, and all space was gathered up in the small bare cabin where they danced.

Heyward knew the "shouters" well, and was so accustomed to these strange rhythms since boyhood that he found little remarkable in them, though he was incapable of joining them. He was thunderstruck when Gershwin started "shouting" with them, throwing himself with all his energy into the strange dance, performing so well that he was accepted among them and given the foremost place. "I think," said Heyward afterwards, "he is probably the only white man in America who could have done that."

In fact many white men could have done it. In New York there were many Jews belonging to the Chassidic movement which came to birth in Poland and Russia about the time of the American Revolution. After centuries of oppression they abandoned orthodox ritual and substituted the direct mystical approach to God by means of song and dance, following the precept of the *Zohar* that "heaven is best approached by song". In wild rapture, with frenzied chants and acclamations, they too danced and stamped their feet and whirled in close unison until they reached a state of divine abandonment, when God seemed to be present to them.

The roots of many of the melodies and nearly all the most haunting passages of *Porgy and Bess* can be traced to Chassidic sources mingled with Gullah. The burial scene in the opera derives its power from ancient Jewish laments. Porgy is not wholly Negro. There are times when he wears the face of a young Jewish exile singing the Lord's song in a strange land.

Unkempt, with a three-days' growth of beard, soaking up atmosphere and colour from the Gullah Negroes, always wandering about in his swim-suit, pounding out new melodies on the battered piano which had been imported from Charleston, Gershwin was in his element. He was deeply suntanned, living in a state of physical and spiritual euphoria. He was gracious and kind, and the old restlessness seemed to have left him. He complained only when the insects hurled themselves against the window screens at night, filling the air with their strenuous piping.

Here for the first time since the days of his childhood he found himself in a world stripped to its essentials: a tottering beach-house on the waterfront, palms, sand and sea. Social conventions were meaningless on the island. There were no telephones. He was under no compulsion to please and entertain. For the first and last time in his life, as a mature man, he lived beyond the reaches of sophistication. He found himself in the beach-house, and wrote some of his best and most enduring music. Perhaps mercifully the house can never be transformed into a musical museum. It was blown out to sea in the next hurricane.

He returned to New York with months of work in front of him. By September he had completed the orchestration of the second scene of Act One. Even with the help of the Schillinger method of composition, which gave a mathematical richness and depth to the work, he was unable to complete it in less than a year of intense concentration. Kay Swift and others were called in to help. "He liked to bounce the music off people," she recalled recently. "We rasped through the various songs for him while he worked, never changing the keys to make it easier for us. But none of us doubted for a minute that this was a masterpiece."

The man in the swim-suit was exchanged for the restless New York sophisticate, who wandered to Fire Island, White Plains, and Palm Beach to put the finishing touches to the composition. Schillinger kept a watchful eye on him, studying the score as it progressed and occasionally suggesting minor changes. Kay Swift, singing herself hoarse for a year, regarded herself as one of the luckiest people alive for having watched a masterpiece come to birth. Heyward, too, was contented, and his letters to Gershwin at the time shine with his pleasure.

It is Gershwin's *Porgy and Bess*, but many people had a hand in it. The libretto was entirely Heyward's, and so were most of the lyrics. Of the more famous songs Heyward wrote "Summertime", "A Woman is a Sometime Thing", "The Buzzard Song", and "It Takes a Long Pull to Get There". Heyward also wrote the prayer in the hurricane scene: "Oh, de Lawd Shake de Heavens, and de Lord Rock the Ground." Ira wrote "It Ain't Necessarily So" and "There's a Boat Dat's Leavin' Soon for New York".

"I Got Plenty o' Nuttin' " was written by Ira and Heyward in collaboration.

At last on September 2, 1935, the work was finished, and Gershwin breathed a sigh of relief. It was a vast work, amounting to 559 pages in the published score, and every note of the orchestration came from his own pen. *Porgy and Bess* is almost continuous music, and all of it was his.

He was bubbling all over with enthusiasm. One day he was walking in the street with the score under his arm when he met Vinton Freedley. He laughed, pointed to seventeen pages of the clarinet parts, and shouted, "Look what I've done!" He showed the same excitement to everyone. He played the "crap game" fugue from the opening of *Porgy and Bess*. His face was beaming. "Get this," he exclaimed. "Gershwin writing fugues! What will the boys say next?"

In those days he seemed to be living in a state of euphoria. Vernon Duke accompanied him to Boston for the tryout. Gershwin beamed through the rehearsals. One day Vernon Duke was sitting in the last row of the orchestra when he suddenly felt two powerful hands gripping him by the shoulders. "Hey, Dukie," Gershwin whispered fiercely. "Just listen to those overtones!"

Many similar stories are told about Gershwin's behaviour at this time. He had reached a pitch of excitement so intense, and so exhilarating to those around him, that he seemed in some strange way to be at once a sky-larking child and a musician of fantastic accomplishment awe-struck by his own music. In him overweening pride and humility achieved a happy marriage.

He worked prodigiously through the rehearsals, for there was still some music to be written and many changes were made. He auditioned all the main characters, choosing Anne Brown to play Bess, Todd Duncan to play Porgy, and John W. Bubbles to play Sportin' Life, the Mephistophelean "giver of life". Bubbles was one half of the tap-dance team Buck and Bubbles, and had to be coaxed into his rôle with tap-dancing suitable to the songs he had to sing. Todd Duncan was big, broad-faced and always smiling, a natural singer, a bass baritone of remarkable power, a former concert singer and teacher of music at Howard University. The opera was off to a good start.

There was some rivalry between Rouben Mamoulian, the director, and Gershwin, for while each admitted and proclaimed the brilliance of the other, and they were perfectly prepared to share the limelight, there were inevitable quarrels. Rouben Mamoulian, fresh from his successes in Hollywood, could never quite forget that he had seen an entirely different Gershwin at their first meeting in 1923. In those days Gershwin did not yet wear the halo of success. "He was a very worried young man," Mamoulian remembered, "very ambitious and not very happy. Rather reserved and self-centred and in some curious way suspicious of the world." Gershwin was no longer suspicious of the world. He was enjoying himself as he had never enjoyed himself before.

There were six weeks of rehearsals, and four days after Gershwin's thirty-seventh birthday, on September 30, 1935, the world premier of *Porgy and Bess* opened in Boston. Ten days later came the New York opening at the Alvin Theatre, with some of the songs cut and a good deal of stage business omitted, for Boston had shown that the original production was altogether too long by about an hour and ten minutes. Mamoulian and Gershwin were still rivals: those who were present at the opening night remember their simultaneous rush to the stage to take their bows.

Porgy and Bess had come to stay. Henceforth they were to belong to American musical tradition, to be remembered as long as American songs were sung. But there was no universal acclamation from the critics. Music critics revelled in the music, drama critics revelled in the drama, or did not revel. Olin Downes said the music was unworthy of the emotional intensity and veracity of the play, and he found in the music little relevance to dramatic situation and no comparable strength of feeling. Virgil Thomson described it as "crooked opera and half-way folklore". Many pointed to the strange hybrid mixture of Broadway entertainment, opera, and play. There was a general feeling of uneasiness—it played too slowly, or the music was too syrupy, or too many hurdles were being crossed. No one disputed that there were good and wonderful things in it, but people wondered whether they would endure.

Porgy and Bess was a commercial failure. It ran for only 124 performances in New York, and failed to earn its running expenses and its initial cost of $70,000. Gershwin and DuBose Heyward each lost the money they had invested in it. The sixteen weeks in New York were followed by a three-month road tour, but nothing happened during the tour to suggest that it would ever arise from the obscurity into which it was falling. When Gershwin died less than two years later and an inventory was made of his estate, valued at over $200,000, his interest in *Porgy and Bess* was given an evaluation of $20,000 against a presumptive sale of the film rights, so little appeal did it seem to have at the time.

But *Porgy and Bess* was not headed for oblivion. The play possessed, even in its musical form, a raw naked strength; the music included the best songs Gershwin had written. When Cheryl Crawford revived it in 1941, turning most of the recitatives into speech, so speeding up the action, it played for eight months in New York and went on tour through twenty-six cities. With the recitatives omitted, Gershwin's music came into focus; and Virgil Thomson, who had previously described it as "crooked opera and half-way folklore", reversed his opinion, and described it as "a beautiful piece of music and a deeply moving play for the lyric theatre". And since under Cheryl Crawford's direction the new version had a sweep and pace lacking in the old, it is just possible that Virgil Thomson's judgements were equally just.

The triumph of *Porgy and Bess* was only beginning. It played in the Danish Royal Opera in Copenhagen during the German occupation with an all-Danish cast; and the Danish underground took savage delight in broadcasting, "It Ain't Necessarily So" after each announcement of a Nazi victory. It was played in Moscow in May, 1945 by the Stanislavsky Players, and a month later at the Zurich festival of music. Thereafter it was seen and heard in nearly every country of Europe. It was seen in Stockholm, Gothenburg, Berlin, Venice, Belgrade, Athens, Naples, Milan, Rome, Turin, Marseilles, Paris, Antwerp. It was shown all over South America, and behind the Iron Curtain. In 1956 it reached Moscow, and went on to play at the Warsaw Opera House. In four years it played in twenty-nine countries, and its journeys have only begun. In 1959 it became a wide-screen technicolor film with Sidney Poitier playing the rôle of Porgy and Dorothy Dandridge playing Bess. Though the film was a lavish extravaganza, drowned in gelatine colour, all the raw edges smoothed over, with Catfish Row hovering in a shimmering haze and Sidney Poitier so theatrically handsome that it was inconceivable that he could ever suggest a decrepit beggar, even then something of the savagery of the play came through. Not even the screen could destroy the indestructible quality of the play.

Gershwin never knew his greatest triumph. Worn out, he left for Hollywood to recoup his fortunes, and those who saw him go spoke of a curious change in his manner. He seemed to have aged a little; to be growing wiser; to be kinder. The ebullience had gone, and when he spoke of Hollywood, he laughed nervously and said, "I'll take their money, and put it back into writing good opera." He planned to write another opera with DuBose Heyward based on his novel, *Star-spangled Virgin*, which had a Virgin Island theme. He had many other plans, and was always talking about returning quickly to New York.

In Hollywood he wrote the songs and music for the Ginger Rogers–Fred Astaire musical *Shall We Dance?* and went on to write another musical for Fred Astaire and Joan Fontaine. Both scores were written under pressure, and since he wrote best under pressure, he was able to produce memorable songs including "A Foggy Day", and "Nice Work If You Can Get it". He was planning to return to New York when Samuel Goldwyn invited him to compose the music for *The Goldwyn Follies*. He never came home.

9

Death and Resurrection

IN HOLLYWOOD he had never been gayer, happier, or more in command of himself. He gave the impression of a man completely at peace with himself, riding himself hard, but knowing when to rest, swimming, painting, playing tennis, visiting the houses of film stars and inviting them to his own house; and he quite frankly enjoyed the spectacle of the most beautiful women in the world reclining in bathing suits around his swimming pool.

Film music came effortlessly to him. He enjoyed working on *The Goldwyn Follies*, and with George Balanchine he planned a ballet based on *An American in Paris*. He had other plans. Lynn Riggs was writing the libretto of an opera for him. He was busy with a string quartet based on themes he had heard among the Gullahs, when he was staying at Folly Island with DuBose Heyward. The quartet, with its fast opening movement followed by an extremely slow second movement, was already finished in his head, and he spoke of renting a small cabin in Coldwater Canyon where he could write it down at leisure, without interruptions. He told Merle Armitage that he intended to start on the quartet as soon as he had completed the music for *The Goldwyn Follies*. "It's going through my head all the time," he said. "It's about to drive me crazy, I'm so damned full of new ideas!"

There was nothing, of course, unusual in this: he had always been gripped by new ideas, and a constant stream of music was flowing through his mind. No one paid any attention when he said it was driving him crazy. He had never shown the least sign of being crazy.

He was at the height of his fame, and enjoying every moment of it. He enjoyed flying across the country—to Portland, Seattle, St. Louis, and Detroit—performing his own works to standing-room-only audiences. Composing as effortlessly as ever and earning a fabulous income from his film music, he was still a little amused by himself, and he still liked to talk about himself in the third person. "Gershwin's music is terrific," he said, and no one doubted it.

Happy, impulsive, bubbling over with good health, without worries of any kind, he was sailing through life in an iridescent haze of music. It was remembered afterwards that he was a little more restless than usual, but he was no more restless than most of the people who work in Hollywood. Occasionally his temper snapped and there were brief flurries of petulance, and these too could be put down to the enervating climate of California.

Even when he complained of his health, no one paid much attention. He had always suffered from stomach trouble, but it was remembered that he had been a hypochondriac for twenty years and no one took his sufferings very seriously. It annoyed him that his hair was thinning out, and he bought an electric massage machine and for half an hour every morning submitted himself to scalp treatment. The machine employed rotating suction pads which brought a rush of blood to his head, and he liked to think that his hair was growing back again. It is just possible that the machine was responsible for the brain tumour from which he died.

The first warning that anything was wrong came on the night of February 10th, when he was making his first appearance as a soloist with the Los Angeles Philharmonic in an all-Gershwin programme. It was a gala performance, with the seats sold out weeks before. Gershwin had been in good form during the rehearsals, and he was especially delighted by a reception given for him just before the concert at the Hollywood-Plaza Hotel. His friends were in the audience. He played brilliantly, and only a very few people observed that he fumbled an easy passage in the first movement of his *Concerto in F*, and fumbled again in the coda. The conductor, Alexander Smallens, noticed it and covered up for him. After the performance Oscar Levant went to see him backstage. "I was thinking of you when I made those mistakes," Gershwin said mysteriously. To others he admitted that his mind had gone absolutely blank and for a few seconds he had had to fight his way through a wall of terrifying darkness.

There was another performance the following night. While he was conducting he was assailed by a sensation he had never known: he had an ear-splitting headache and at the same time there was the smell of burning rubber in his nostrils. He was shaken, but continued conducting. The headache and the smell of burning rubber seemed in some way inextricably combined.

There was nothing outwardly wrong with his health, no failure of muscular co-ordination. He worked, went to parties, played tennis and took his daily six-mile walk in the Hollywood hills. He looked bronzed and fit, and the doctors who examined him could think of no other explanation for the blackouts than overwork. It is not unusual for a musician to have momentary blackouts. What was unusual and frightening was the smell of burning rubber, and the knowledge that it might come again.

Gershwin was inclined to make light of it. There might be some quite normal physical explanation. He was too busy and too happy to pay much attention to a momentary lapse during a concert. February passed. There was no recurrence of the strange experience until April. He was sitting in a barber-shop in Beverly Hills when the stabbing headache came again, and the smell of burning rubber. Frightened, nauseated, he made his way in a daze to the house on Roxbury Drive.

It was the beginning of the end. He went through the motions of living, composing every day, playing tennis every day, but his strength was ebbing. He was often listless. By June it was obvious that he was seriously ill. He slept soundly, but when he woke up he could only dress himself with difficulty. The early part of the day was the worst: he would sit on the edge of the bed, staring into the distance, his eyes glazed, his hands lying limp on his lap. He complained about the brightness of the light, and for long hours he remained in his bedroom with the shades drawn, demanding absolute quietness. The doctor examined him. Heart, lungs, nervous reflexes—there was nothing wrong. All the doctors could find was that he had lost the sense of smell in one nasal passage.

Listless in the mornings, he would slowly, as with an immense effort, emerge from his silence in the afternoon, and by evening he was himself again. He still went to parties, where it was noticed that he kept spilling and dropping things. He still sat down at the piano and played for friends, but the old fire had gone from him. He could be gay and entertaining, but gave the impression of playing a rôle. In the midst of parties with his oldest friends, black moods descended on him. He became bitter and argumentative, taking offence easily; and since he was not the kind of person who had ever taken offence easily or ever engaged in bitter arguments, it was generally agreed that he was in need of a holiday. On June 12th he went off for a few days' vacation in Coronada. When he returned he seemed to be well on the road to recovery.

On Sunday, June 20th, he awoke with the worst headache he had known up to this time. The doctor came and tested him for a brain tumour, calling in a neurologist and an eye specialist. All agreed that the symptoms suggested the presence of a tumour. Gershwin refused to believe that he was the victim of anything so serious, and burst out laughing. "There's nothing wrong with me," he exclaimed. "I'm just overworked, exhausted."

As a precaution it was decided to send him to Cedars of Lebanon Hospital for a complete physical check-up, with a complicated series of tests. These lasted four days, from June 23rd to June 26th. He refused to take a spinal test, which usually results in severe headaches, because he was already suffering from a headache so strong that it was driving him to the verge of madness. All the tests proved negative. According to the doctors he was healthy in every respect, and there was no rational explanation for the headaches.

The psychiatrists were called in, for it was thought by some doctors that the headaches were due to some mental disturbance, and they might vanish once the cause of the disturbance was known. In New York he had undergone a year's analysis with Dr. Gregory Zilboorg, but he was not a very co-operative patient, he had broken off the analysis suddenly, and he had not felt a great need for it. The famous psychiatrist, Dr. Ernest Simmel, was approached, and after comparing notes with Dr. Zilboorg, he took charge. His first step was to order a change of residence, and Gershwin was accordingly taken to live in the house of Erwin Harburg, who was then leaving Hollywood for New York. It was a much smaller and quieter house. There was no telephone. Here he could be sheltered, and gradually warmed back to life.

Most of the day he slept like a sick child, very quiet and undemonstrative in the rare intervals when he was awake. There were fewer headaches, but the listlessness remained. He was living in a remote world, almost unreachable. Ira visited him, and three doctors called on him every day to test his reflexes, examine his eyes and search for symptoms of a brain tumour, which by this time had become the only logical explanation of his extraordinary behaviour. George Balanchine found him in bed in a dark room, talking with difficulty in a strange faraway voice, intelligible but barely audible.

During the morning of Friday, July 9th, his illness reached a desperate stage. Dr. Simmel, who was spending the afternoon with him, asked him to play the *Rhapsody in Blue*, but as soon as he sat down at the piano, it became clear that his co-ordination was gone. Ira was summoned to the house, to decide on what action should be taken. He could only stand upright with difficulty; and there was a terrifying strangeness about all his movements. He already wore the look of a man about to die, very gentle and withdrawn, speaking in that strange faraway voice. At five o'clock in the afternoon he became drowsy and fell asleep. They wrapped a bathrobe round him, called an ambulance and took him to Cedars of Lebanon Hospital for the second time.

The doctors had finally come to the conclusion that he was suffering without any doubt from a brain tumour, and must be operated on immediately.

A great deal of time had been wasted, and it was necessary to act quickly. That night Gershwin was kept under observation. Nothing was done until the next day.

Ira hoped that Dr. Harvey Cushing, the greatest living brain surgeon, could be brought to Hollywood quickly, but this was found to be impossible. The doctors at the hospital suggested Dr. Walter Danby, a former student of Cushing and one of the country's top brain surgeons, but many hours passed before he could be found—he was vacationing on a yacht in Chesapeake Bay with the Governor of Maryland. George Pallay, one of Gershwin's closest and oldest friends, in desperation called the White House, which in turn called the Coast Guard. Two destroyers were sent to Chesapeake Bay to find the doctor, who was then flown to Newark, New Jersey, and an open wire was kept for him so that he could follow the course of the operation, since it was obviously too late for him to fly to California.

Gershwin was already sinking when the operation began at 10.30 p.m. His pulse was low, and he wore the look of a man who no longer wants to fight for his life. Dr. Carl Rand of the Cedars of Lebanon Hospital performed the operation, with three more doctors in attendance. Gershwin's head was shaved and a small window was opened in the skull to allow the surgeons to probe for the exact location of the tumour. They found it at last in the right temporal lobe of the brain: it was a very large tumour, with a cystic growth which was almost certainly the cause of the violent headaches. The operation lasted four hours, and as it progressed reports were telephoned to Dr. Danby in Newark, who gave his blessing and approval to the four doctors. Finally, the tumour was removed, the window in the head was sealed, and the patient was wheeled out from the operating theatre. In private the doctors held out little hope for recovery. The operation had taken place too late, and involved cutting into an extremely sensitive part of the brain. If he ever awoke from his deep sleep, it was possible that he would be a drivelling idiot, incapable of understanding a bar of music.

In the hospital his friends waited. Moss Hart, Oscar Levant, Arthur Kober, and Elizabeth Meyer were there; so of course were Ira and his wife, Leonore. At daybreak they left, all of them believing there was a faint possibility of recovery.

He never recovered consciousness. His head bandaged, pale and drawn, his breathing coming with increasing difficulty, he died quietly at 10.35 on the following morning, July 11, 1937. He was thirty-eight years old.

Living, he had been a symbol of his time, a man a little larger than life because he concentrated in himself so many of the passions of his time. Dead, he became a legend.

How legendary he became at the moment of dying was witnessed by the outpouring of grief and the black headlines. People who had never set eyes on him and who had heard his music only on the radio felt as though they had received a physical wound. To them he represented the youth and gaiety of the twenties and thirties; and with his going, the air seemed colder.

His body, in a hermetically sealed coffin, was brought to New York, and 3,500 people attended the funeral service at Temple Emanu-El on Fifth Avenue. The service opened with a Bach aria and the Bach chorale "Come sweetest death", and a string quartet played Beethoven's deeply religious posthumous Concerto Opus 130. Rabbi Stephen S. Wise delivered the eulogy, celebrating him as "the singer of the songs of America's soul". The flower-covered coffin left the temple to the music of the Andante section of the *Rhapsody in Blue*. It was July 15th, but a cold rain

Fred Astaire, George Gershwin and Ira Gershwin rehearse *Shall We Dance*, July 1937

Self-portrait

was falling that day; and the cortege went to the cemetery while heavy clouds swept across Manhattan.

Fiorello La Guardia was there, wearing a top hat, looking strangely pale and ill-at-ease in the company of former Mayor James Walker. George M. Cohan, Al Jolson, Vernon Duke, Walter Damrosch, Gene Buck, and Edwin Franko Goldman were the honorary pall-bearers. As they huddled in the rain outside the Temple Emanu-El, all of them felt that something preposterous and beyond their comprehension had happened. Men could not —should not—die when they are at the height of their creative powers.

The Spaniards were at war, Hitler was about to march into Austria, and two years later all Europe was in flames.

George Gershwin died at the age of thirty-eight, with all his best work before him. His claim to fame does not lie in the fact that he elevated jazz to the height where it could be regarded as serious music, nor did it lie in his breathtaking facility of invention. His real claim to fame is to be found in history, in that history which is rarely written because it records the heartbeats, the dreams, the secrets, the private griefs and joys of an age.

If we knew the songs the girls sang in the fields of ancient Athens, we would know far more than we shall ever know about the spirit of those times. We know the songs that were sung in the twenties and thirties, and we can measure to a hairbreadth the spirit of those two decades. His music with its leaping discords and menacing gaiety, frail as glass, lusty as youth, perfectly mirrored the age he lived in. He caught the mood of his time, and having crystallized it, he stamped it with his own image. In the history of the American imagination he has a secure place.

He had advantages denied to greater musicians. He came to fruition at a time when everything seemed to be working in his favour. Radio and phonographs immeasurably increased his audience. Silent films gave way to sound when he was at the height of his popularity. All the vehicles of mass entertainment welcomed him with open arms; and no musician was ever photographed so much or saw himself so often in the newspapers. There seemed to be a conspiracy to assist his progress.

When a man becomes famous above so many millions of his fellows, there are always good reasons. The soap opera novelist, whose work hits the best-seller lists, is not altogether to be despised: he has answered the unspoken needs of many and recorded some fragment of the truth. Gershwin deliberately aimed for popularity and never for a moment forgot his need to improve his bank balance. He was not one of those who write music for the sake of music. It never occurred to him that he was wasting his time when he went to Hollywood. He never went into the wilderness, and it is significant that his greatest works, the second movement of the *Concerto in F* and *Porgy and Bess*, were begun in the comparative obscurity of a shack at Chautauqua and on an island off the Charleston coast, far from the temptations of New York, in remote places where he could be alone with himself.

Like Thomas Wolfe who died at thirty-seven, and Scott Fitzgerald who died at forty-four, he seemed to be endowed with eternal youth. He had the gifts of youth, and the prodigality of youth, and seems never to have quite grown up. Strangely, photographs taken during the last year of his life show very little change from those taken when he was twenty. There was always the same blandness, the same slightly surprised air of the perpetual undergraduate, the long, handsome, streamlined face always unlined. He seemed to have no inner life; he was a surface, reflecting the colours of things. Sometimes the colours of the world, as though of their own accord, penetrated below the surface and he was able to reproduce them with an exquisite tact and a kind of innocence which demands the highest degree of honesty in a man.

He was a voice, an embodiment of an age, working at a time when it was still possible to speak with an authentic voice on a single theme. In those days the air did not smell of the smoke from the incinerators; and the world, though corrupt, was not yet as corrupted as it became. In that landscape he walked easily, rarely knowing where he was going, for a sense of direction was rare in the twenties and thirties, and why should one hurry in any particular direction when all the prospects are pleasing? He took the easier roads, when he might have done a greater service to music if he had climbed some mountains.

So to the end he remained a child of his time, mildly ingenuous, very knowledgeable, delighting in the pleasures which the world set before him while rarely able to enjoy them, possessed of vast competence and some sparks of genius, and strangely indifferent to his fellow men. He was so wasteful of his talents that he spent hardly more than three years of his working life on work that was worthy of him. He lived in great poverty and great wealth, and seems never to have known what it was to live as ordinary human beings live. The man who wrote countless love songs was always complaining that he never knew how to love. He never knew suffering. Even at the very end suffering was mercifully withheld from him, as he withdrew into the twilight madness from which he escaped only in the operating theatre. All his life he lived youthfully; then in one terrible week he became a drivelling old man; and then it was over. Knowing the manner of man he was, he was perhaps as lucky in his dying as he was in his life.

It is no service to his memory to paint him in the colours of a Horatio Alger story. The young, vibrant hero of American music wore as many scars as Lindbergh, the only other hero of his time comparable to him. We can no longer say, as Gilbert Seldes said at the time of his death, "One had forgotten that there still existed in the world a force so boundless, an exaltation so high, that anyone could storm heaven with cheers and laughter," for we know now that Gershwin stormed heaven only at his leisure and there was very little laughter in the enterprise.

Gershwin remains a towering figure, but not for the reasons which are usually given. More than most he suffered from the sickness of his age, and went blindly after the rewards so copiously offered him. He will be remembered as the mirror of his time, as the brilliant composer of the *Rhapsody in Blue*, the *Concerto in F* and *Porgy and Bess*, a musician who at his best either consciously or unconsciously drew his inspiration from the deep wells of Jewish lamentation.

Select Bibliography

Armitage, Merle, *Gershwin, Man and Legend*. New York: Duell, Sloan & Pearce, 1958.

——, *George Gershwin*. London: Longmans, Green, 1938.

Cowell, Henry, ed., *American Composers on American Music*. Palo Alto: Stanford University Press, 1933.

Durham, Frank, *DuBose Heyward, the Man Who Wrote Porgy*. Columbia: University of South Carolina Press, 1954.

Ewen, David, *A Journey to Greatness*. New York: Henry Holt, 1954.

Goldberg, Isaac, *George Gershwin, a Study in American Music*. New York: Frederick Ungar, 1958.

Jablonski, Edward, and Lawrence D. Stewart, *The Gershwin Years*. New York: Doubleday & Company, 1958.

Levant, Oscar, *A Smattering of Ignorance*. New York: Doubleday & Company, 1940.

Van Vechten, Carl, *Peter Whiffle*. New York: Alfred A. Knopf, 1924.

Select Discography

(Available in the lists of British gramophone record companies at the time of going to press; the numbers refer to ordinary LP or EP records, but in many cases stereo versions are also issued. The letter R indicates the reverse of the record.)

An American in Paris

Leonard Bernstein and the Philharmonic-Symphony Orchestra of New York (R. Rhapsody in Blue—see below)	Phillips ABL 3232
Leonard Pennario (piano) with the Hollywood Bowl Symphony Orchestra, conductor: Felix Slatin (R. Rhapsody in Blue—see below)	Capitol P 8343

Concerto in F for Piano and Orchestra (New York Concerto)

Julius Katchen (piano) with the Mantovani Orchestra (R. Rhapsody in Blue—see below)	Decca LXT 5068

Porgy and Bess

Complete Opera (3 records)	Phillips NBL 5016/8
Film Sound Track	Phillips ABL 3282
Lena Horne and Harry Belafonte (Selections)	RCA RD 25129
Ella Fitzgerald and Louis Armstrong (2 records—album set)	HMV CLP 1245/6
Miles Davis Quintet (Selections)	Fontana TFL 5056

Rhapsody in Blue

George Gershwin himself (piano) and other piano pieces with conversation at a rehearsal	Ember EMB 3315
Leonard Bernstein and the Philharmonic-Symphony Orchestra of New York (R. An American in Paris—see above)	Phillips ABL 3232
Leonard Pennario (piano) with the Hollywood Bowl Symphony Orchestra, conductor: Felix Slatin (R. An American in Paris—see above)	Capitol P 8343
Julius Katchen (piano) with the Mantovani Orchestra (R. Concerto in F—see above)	Decca LXT 5068

Songs and Individual Numbers from Shows and Films

The Gershwin Years (3 records—album set) The George Bassman Orchestra	Brunswick LAT 8315/7
Ella Fitzgerald Sings Gershwin (5 records) with Nelson Riddle's Orchestra	HMV CLP 1338/9 CLP 1347/8 CLP 1353
Mr. Wilson and Mr. Gershwin The Teddy Wilson Trio	Phillips BBL 7344
Ella Fitzgerald and Louis Armstrong Part of *Ella and Louis*	HMV CLP 1098
Part of *Ella and Louis Again* (Vol. I)	HMV CLP 1146
Part of *Ella and Louis Again* (Vol. II)	HMV CLP 1147
A Foggy Day Dave Brubeck Quartet	part of Vogue LAE 12114
Frank Sinatra	part of Capitol W 587

SELECT DISCOGRAPHY

Fred Astaire   part of London HAR 2219

But Not for Me
  Billie Holiday   part of HMV 7eg 8627

Embraceable You
  Frank Sinatra   part of Fontana TLF 5082 and tfe 17286

I Got Rhythm
  Kid Ory—Red Allen Orchestra   part of HMV CLP 1422

Lady Be Good
  Errol Garner   part of Mercury Emarcy MMB 12010

  Lester Young with Count Basie's Orchestra   part of Fontana TFL 5065

  Fred Astaire   part of London HAR 2219

  Benny Goodman Trio   part of RCA rcx 1033

Let's Call the Whole Thing Off
  Billie Holiday   part of Columbia 33CX 10145

Love is Here to Stay
  Billie Holiday   part of HMV 7eg 8627

SELECT DISCOGRAPHY

 Lionel Hampton Orchestra   part of Phillips BBL 7444

Nice Work if You Can Get It
 Billie Holiday   part of Fontana TFL 5106

The Man I Love
 Miles Davis and the Modern Jazz Giants   part of Esquire 32—100

 Benny Goodman Orchestra   part of Phillips BBL 7441

 Art Tatum   part of Fontana tfe 17236

They All Laughed
 George Shearing   part of MGM ep 718

 Fred Astaire   part of London HAR 2219

 Bing Crosby   part of HMV 7eg 8475

They Can't Take That Away From Me
 Stan Getz   part of HMV CLP 1351

 Frank Sinatra   part of Capitol W 587

 Fred Astaire   part of London HAR 2219

Compiled by Peter Watt
Discography © A. P. F. Watt 1961

Index

Aarons, Alex, 36, 75
Absinthe Drinker, The, 71
Aeolian Hall, 44, 46, 48
Alger, Horatio, 13, 40, 115
Also sprach Zarathustra, 45
Alvin Theatre, 104
American Composers on American Music, 67 f.n.
American folk-music, 66–7
American In Paris, An, 74–81, 83, 84, 89, 97, 107
Annie Laurie, 21
An-ski, S., 74
Armitage, Merle, 107
Astaire, Fred, 106
Atkinson, Brooks, 36
Atlantic City, 45, 89
Auric, Georges, 73
Austria, 74, 75, 113

Bach, 58, 112
Balanchine, George, 107, 111
Barnes, Maggie, 93, 94
Bartok, 44
Baton, Rhené, 73
Bayes, Nora, 34–5
Beethoven, 24, 54, 58, 77, 112
  Concerto Opus 130, 112
  Missa Solemnis, 77
Bellini, 44
Bellows, George, 71
Benton, Thomas Hart, 71
Berlin, Irving, 30, 31, 35, 40, 44, 46, 48
Between Two Worlds, 74–5
Beverly Hills, 109
Beyer (*Exercises*), 24
Billy the Kidd, 93

Black Bottom, the, 40
Blue Monday, 42–3
"Blues", 28, 46, 47, 48, 50, 54, 64, 66, 74, 76, 89
Bolitho, William, 84
Bolton, Guy, 85
Boston, 47, 103, 104
Boston Evening Transcript, 36–7, 88
Boston Symphony Orchestra, 88
Botkin, Henry, 58, 68, 70, 99
Bridge of San Luis Rey, The, 72
Broadway, 35, 36, 40, 41, 43, 83–6, 91, 104
Brooklyn, 62
Brown, Anne, 103
  John Mason, 90–1
Brownsville, 18
Bruskin, Rose, 20, 31, 57, 82
Bubbles, John W., 103
Buck, Gene, 113

Caesar, Irving, 37, 38
California, 45, 108, 111
Capitol Theatre, 38
Carnegie Hall, 55, 67, 74, 75, 77, 85
Case of Sergeant Grischa, The, 72
Cedars of Lebanon Hospital, 110–111
Century Theatre, 33, 34
Chagall, 71
Charleston, the, 40, 54
Charleston, 93–4, 98, 101, 114
Chautauqua, 53, 114
Chesapeake Bay, 111
Chopin, 25, 50
Christadora House, 26
Clark, Emily, 61

Cohan, George M., 113
Coldwater Canyon, 107
Columbia, 57
  University, Trustees of, 91
Communism, 91
Concerto in F, 53–5, 67, 73, 81, 108, 114, 115
Constantinople, 38, 58
Cook, Joe, 35–7
Coolidge, Calvin, 72
Copenhagen, 105
Coward, Noel, 60, 68, 76
Cowell, Henry, 64–7
Craig, Gordon, 68
Crawford, Cheryl, 105
Cuba, 88–9
Cuban Overture, 89
Cushing, Dr. Harvey, 111

Daly, Bill, 58
Damrosch, Walter, 47, 74, 75, 113
Danby, Dr. Walter, 111–12
Dandridge, Dorothy, 105
Danish Royal Opera, 105
Debussy, 25, 50, 54, 75, 77
Declaration of Independence, 95
Deep South, the, 37
Delicious, 87
Dérain, 71
De Sylva, Buddy, 42, 45
Devereaux, Diana, 90
Diaghilev, 73
Die Fledermaus, 75
Dixie, 39
Dolin, Anton, 73
Donaldson, Walter, 44
Downes, Olin, 49, 55, 104
Dreiser, Theodore, 61
Dresser, Louise, 34
Dreyfus, Max, 34–5, 38, 40, 58
Duke Ellington Band, 83
Duke, Vernon, 38, 51, 58–9, 68, 73, 76, 103, 113

Duncan, Isadora, 68
Duncan, Todd, 103
Durante, Jimmy, 83
Dvořák's *Humoresque*, 23, 24
Dybbuk, The, 74–5

East Side, 15, 20, 22, 26, 82, 100
Elgar, Sir Edward (*Pomp and Circumstance*), 48
Elman, Mischa, 47
England, 16, 52, 68, 72
Ernst, Hugh, 48
Europe, 45, 71, 72–81, 97, 113
  Eastern, 16
"Experiment in Modern Music", 51

Farrar, John, 94
Farrell, Patric, 70
Fascism, 91
Ferber, Edna, 97
Fields, Lew, 33
Film-music, 107
Fire Island, 102
Fitzgerald, Ella, 53
Fitzgerald, F. Scott, 79, 114
Fletcher, Horace J., 84
Follies, The Goldwyn, 106–7
Folly Beach, 99–100
  Island, 107
Fontaine, Joan, 106
Foster, Stephen, 37
Fourteenth Rhapsody, 45
Fox film, 87
Foy, Eddie, 83
France, 52, 73
Freedley, Vinton, 75, 85, 103
Funny Face, 67

Gauguin, 71
Gauthier, Eva, 44
Gaxton, William, 90
Germany, 52, 74

INDEX

Gershwin, Ira (Isidore or Israel), 57–9, 64, 70, 73, 83, 91, 98, 102, 110, 111, 112
  Frances, 73
  Morris, 18–21, 57, 58, 82–3
Gershovitz, Moshe, see Gershwin, Morris
  Yacob (Gershwin, George), 20ff
Gilbert and Sullivan operas, 21, 91
Gilman, Lawrence, 50, 55
Girl Crazy, 85–7
Girl from Utah, The, 30
Glaenzer, Jules, 58–60, 79
Glazounov (Fifth Symphony), 55
"Goat Sammy", 93–4
Godowsky, 47
Goldberg, Isaac, 38, 50, 67
Goldfaden, Abraham, 31–2
Goldfarb, 24
Goldman, Edwin Franko, 113
Goldwyn, Samuel, 106
Gorman, Ross, 48
Graf Zeppelin (airship), 72
Grand Street Theatre, 16
"Great Emancipator, the", 89
Great Gatsby, The, 63
Grofe, Ferdinand Rudolph von, 43, 46, 47, 79
Gullahs, 100, 107

Half-past Eight, 36–7
Hambitzer, Charles, 24–6, 31, 41
Hamlet, 16
Hammerstein, Oscar, II, 97
Handel's *Messiah*, 38
Harburg, Erwin, 110
Hardy, Thomas, 80
Harms company, 34, 35
Hart, Moss, 60, 112
Havana, 89
Heifetz, Jascha, 46–7
Hendersonville, 100

Henry Miller Theatre, 37
Herbert, Victor, 33, 46–8
Heyward, Dorothy, 59, 92
  Dubose, 68, 92–107
  Thomas, 95
Hindemith, 44
"Hindustan", 37
Hitler, 62, 72, 113
Hölderlein, Friedrich, 56
Hollywood, 87, 104–111
Hollywood-Plaza Hotel, 108
Howard University, 103

Jazz, 28–9, 32, 40, 42, 44–6, 51, 53, 55, 63, 66–7, 72, 73, 113
Jews, 13–16, 18–21, 26–7, 32, 38–9
Jewish folk-music, 26–7, 38, 43
  opera, 82
  stage, 16, 26, 31
Johnson, James Weldon, 61
Jolson, Al, 38, 83, 97, 113
Juillard, 31

Kahn, Gus, 83
Kahn, Otto, 79
Kalich, Bertha, 16
Kandinsky, 71
Kaufman, George, 89, 91
Kearns, Allen, 86
Keeler, Ruby, 83
Kent, Duke of, 60, 68, 72
Kern, Jerome, 30, 33–5, 40, 44, 97
Kilenyi, Edward, 41
King Lear, 16
"King of Jazz, the", 43, 45–7
"King of Ragtime", 30
Kit Kat Club, 72
Klee, 71
Kober, Arthur, 112
Kokomo, Jimmy, 57
Kokoschka, 71
Koussevitsky, Serge, 62, 64, 88

INDEX

La Bohème, 42
Ladies First, 34
Lady be Good, 51-2, 58
Lady in Red, 35
La Guardia, Fiorello, 113
La La Lucille, 36, 42, 58
Lambert, Constant, 51
"Last Judgement", 70
Lauf der Welt, 45
Lawrence, Gertrude, 60, 67, 68, 72, 75
Léger, 71
Lekeu (*Adagio for Strings*), 75
Let 'Em Eat Cake, 91, 97
Levant, Oscar, 34-5, 62, 70, 80, 108, 112
Lewisohn Stadium, 85, 88
Liebstod, 42
Lindbergh, 63, 115
"Livery Stable Blues", 48
Liszt, 23, 46, 49, 73, 77, 88
    Second Hungarian Rhapsody, 46, 88
London, 51, 52, 60, 68, 72, 81
Love, 89
Los Angeles, 45
    Philharmonic Orchestra, 108
Lost Chord, The, 21

MacDowell Colony, 93
MacGowan, Jack, 85
Mamoulian, Rouben, 103-4
Manhattan Rhapsody, 88
Manhattan Symphony Orchestra, 85
Marche Slav, 45
Maxim's, 60
Maxwell, Elsa, 68, 81
Mayak, the, 38
Mayfair, 68
McCormack, John, 48
Mencken, 63

Merman, Ethel, 86
Metropolitan Opera House, 70
Meyer, Elizabeth, 112
Middleton, George, 74
Milhaud, 44
Miss 1917, 33, 42
"Miss White House", 89
Modern Art, Museum of, New York, 71
Modigliani, 71
Monroe, Harriet, 63
Moore, Dinty, 37
Moore, Victor, 67
Moran, Lois, 90
Moscow, 105
Mountbattens, the, 52, 60, 68, 72
Mozart, 24
Music, 21, 23, 25-8, 38, 41, 43, 48, 51, 58, 65-7, 85, 107, 113, 114
Musical comedies, 15, 26, 30, 32, 45, 51, 52, 54, 75, 83-5, 91
    history of, in U.S.A., 15

National Theatre (American), 31
NBC studios, 87
Negroes, 51, 93-101
Newark, New Jersey, 111, 112
New Orleans, 29
New York, 13ff
    Philharmonic Orchestra, 74
New York Concerto, 53
New York Evening Post, 77
New York Rhapsody, 88
New York Times, 49, 74
New York Tribune, 46
News and Courier, 93

Offenbach, 37, 84
    Barcarolle, 37
    La Duchesse de Gerolstein, 84
Of Thee I Sing, 89-91
Oh Kay, 67, 72
Opera, 42, 75, 93-106

INDEX

"Orange Blossoms in California", 48

Paintings, 68–71
Palais Royal Nightclub, 45, 47
Paley, Lou, 58
Pallay, George, 111
Palm Beach, 102
Paris, 60, 73–6
    opera, 76
Peyser, Herbert, 77
Phonograph, 15, 40, 66, 113
Picasso, 71
Pittsburgh, 34, 62
Poitier, Sidney, 105–6
Porgo, 94
Porgy (book), 69, 92–7
Porgy and Bess, 42, 53, 69, 74, 75, 93–106, 114, 115
    commercial failure, 104
    film of, 105
    story of, 93–6
    triumph, 105–6
Poulenc, Francis, 73
Primrose, 51
Prokofiev, Serge, 73, 78
Pulitzer Prize, 91
Purcell, 44
Pushkin, 58

Rabaud, Henri (*Suite Anglaise*), 55
Rachmaninoff, Serge, 46, 47
Radio, 15, 66, 87, 113
Ragtime, 66
Rand, Dr. Carl, 111
Rappoport, Shloyme Zalmon, 74
Ravel, 72, 73
    Bolero, 72
Rhapsody in Blue, 40–55, 57, 58, 61, 70, 73, 75, 77, 79, 81, 88, 111, 112, 115
Rhapsody in Rivets, 88

Rhumba, 88–9
Riggs, Lynn, 107
Rimsky-Korsakov (*Scheherazade*) 44
Riverside Drive, 37, 57, 59, 68, 70, 86
Robeson, Paul, 61
Rogers, Ginger, 86, 106
Romberg, Sigmund, 33
Rosen, Max (Rosenzweig, M.), 23–4
Rosenfeld, Paul, 77–9
Roth, Murray, 33
Rouault, 70–1
Rousseau, 71
Rubinstein (*Melody in F*), 21, 22
Rubinstein, Beryl, 43–4
Rumshinsky, Joseph, 31
Ryskind, Morrie, 84, 89, 91

Sacher, Madame, 75
San Francisco, 64
Sanborn, Pitts, 50
Santa Barbara, 45
Scandals, 41–3, 45, 51
Schillinger, 102
"Schmaltzy", 40, 89
Schoenberg, 44
Schubert, 66
Second Avenue Theatre, 31, 74
Second Rhapsody, 88
Secunda, Sholom, 31–2
Segal, Vivienne, 33–4
Seldes, George, 44
    Gilbert, 44, 115
"Self-portrait", 69, 71
Show Girl, 83
Simmel, Dr. Ernest, 110–11
Sinbad, 38
Siqueiros, David, 70–1
Smallens, Alexander, 108
Smalls, Samuel, 93–4
Song of the Flame, The, 51–2

Songs, 30ff
Sousa, John Philip, 48
South Carolina, 98–9
Stanislavsky Players, 105
Star-spangled Virgin, 106
Stokowski, 47
Strauss, Frau, 75
 Johann, 75
Stravinsky, Igor, 48, 73–4
Strike up the Band, 83–5, 89, 91
Strunsky, Leonore, 64, 70
"Swanee", 39
Sweet Little Devil, 45–7
Swift, Kay, 58, 61, 68, 102
Switzerland, 84
Syracuse, 36

Taylor, Deems, 44, 49, 75
Tchaikowsky, 50, 77
Television, 15
Tell Me More, 51–2
Temple Emanu-El, 112, 113
Tender Is the Night, 63, 79
Theatre Guild, 92, 97
Théâtre des Champs-Elysées, 73
Théâtre Mogador, 73
The Dial, 44
Thomashefsky, Boris, 15, 31, 32, 74
 Harry, 31
 Thomas, 57
Thompson, Oscar, 77
Thomson, Virgil, 104–5
Tiller girls, 51
Tilzer, Harry von, 33
Tin Pan Alley, 26, 28–39, 43, 67, 85
Tiomkin, Dmitri, 73
Tip Toes, 51–2

Titian, 70
Tony Pastor's Music Hall, 30
Treasure Girl, 75
Tribune, 54
Tristan und Isolde, 42, 98

Varèse, Edgar, 64
Variety, 36
Vaudeville, 29, 30, 34, 58
Vechten, Carl Van, 27, 43, 58, 61–3

Waldorf-Astoria Orchestra, 41
Walker, James, 113
Walküre, Die, 75
Warsaw Opera House, 105
Washington, 84, 89
Watteau, 79
White, George, 41–2, 45, 51
Whiteman, Paul, 43, 45–9, 51
White House, 89, 90
 Plains, 102
Wilder, Thornton, 72
William Tell overture, 24
Winter Gardens, the, 38
Wise, Rabbi Stephen S., 112
Wodehouse, P. G., 33
Wolfe, Thomas, 114
World, the, 42, 44, 50
Wylie, Elinor, 61

Yiddisher Koenig Lear, Der, 16

Ziegfeld, Florenz, 41, 83
Ziegfeld Follies, 41
Zilboorg, Dr. Gregory, 70, 110
Zimbalist, Efrem, 46
Zweig, Arnold, 72

www.ingramcontent.com/pod-product-compliance
Lightning Source LLC
LaVergne TN
LVHW011423080426
835512LV00005B/234